Endorsements

"Life is full of ordinary, mundane, happy, and disappointing moments. Rooted in his own life's journey, Allan Moffat wonderfully opens our eyes and awakens our hearts to the surprising acts of God in these moments and drives home this amazing truth: God loves us, and God loves a good surprise!"

—PHIL WAGLER

Senior Associate Pastor, Gracepoint Community Church

Author of *Kingdom Culture: Growing the Missional Church*

Surrey, British Columbia

"God is alive. And in this book you will meet Him—as Encourager, as Power to change, as loving Father, dearest Friend, and the Hope of mankind. Let your eyes look and your heart be open to this marvellous story of one who walks hand in hand with Him."

—SONYA LUKAITIS

"Readers will find this book instructive and inspirational as they read of a good man's responses to the call of Christ. Allan's story will parallel that of many other people. The book interacts with scripture as a life narrative, not a theological treatise and is very accessible to the average reader.

Allan plainly sets forth the adventure of his faith life with its ups and downs, crises and joys, and rejoices in the faithfulness of God.

I hope *Surprised by God* will have a wide reading."

—REV. BRUCE ROBERTSON
Surrey, British Columbia

SURPRISED BY
GOD

ALLAN W. MOFFAT

SURPRISED BY GOD

ISBN-13: 978-1-77069-081-3

Word Alive Press
131 Cordite Road, Winnipeg, MB R3W 1S1
www.wordalivepress.ca

Library and Archives Canada Cataloguing in Publication

Moffat, Allan W. (Allan Wayne), 1945-
    Surprised by God / written by Allan W. Moffat.

Includes bibliographical references.
ISBN 978-1-77069-081-3

    1. Moffat, Allan W. (Allan Wayne), 1945-. 2. Christian life.
I. Title.

BV4501.3.M638 2010   248.4   C2010-905226-9

I dedicate this book to my wife Beverly who, in her own manner, has demonstrated the love and faithfulness of God to me and has encouraged me greatly in many of my godly endeavours, including the writing and publishing of this book.

Acknowledgements

Most achievements in life are inspired by some significant event or person in our lives. For me, Jason Pankau of Arrow Ministries, USA, through his Omega Course, inspired me to deepen my relationship with God. That, in turn, led to the writing of this book. Thank you, Jason.

Thank you also to my many friends who, having read part or all my efforts, were tremendously encouraging to me. Thank you to Lawrence Swift, John Howat, Vi Rupp, Lorna Parker, Linda Herrmann, Sonja Lukaitis, and Sam Rowland. Each of you has been a tremendous influence.

I would like to further acknowledge Caroline Schmidt, my publishing consultant, and her assistant, Jen Jandavs-Hedlin, for their patient assistance, and also my editor, Evan Braun, who has restored my broken English and poor grammar and made this book something readable.

I must also acknowledge the late Reverend Robert Birch, who was so instrumental in my knowledge of God and my walk with him.

And, most importantly, I acknowledge God himself, who not only gave me the material for this book but inspired me to write it down and share it with each of you.

Foreword

"Nothing surprises me anymore!"

Have you ever said those words? If so, you are not alone.

As a child, I was surprised by almost everything: the beautiful smile of my grade one teacher, two feet of snow on the day of the big math test, even my first taste of salt & vinegar potato chips. Stunning, wonderful and magnificent!

But soon I was grown, and with all that life had thrown my way there was very little that surprised me anymore.

As I read the book that you are holding in your hands, though, I was reminded that there were still thousands of potential surprises to be enjoyed.

I was surprised at how vulnerable Allan Moffat made himself in this book. I was surprised at how deeply his story reached me. And I was surprised at the hope that crept up on me as I read it.

So relax and let Allan's story pour over you.

Oh yes, and one more thing: prepare to be surprised.

—SAM ROWLAND

Musician, Author, and Christian Communicator
Vancouver, Youth for Christ

Table of Contents

Introduction

There are times in everyone's life when, while searching for a particular item, phrase, spouse, or career, we find something different—surprisingly—from what we were looking for. Then there are other times when we find what we're looking for but in a totally different place from where we'd expect to find it. If you take the time right now to search back into the course of your life, you may be surprised to recall several times when you, too, have been unexpectedly surprised.

It may have been that while you were looking for a particular pair of socks in your dresser drawer you discovered a prized earring that you'd given up for lost months or years before.

It may have been that while attending an art show, looking for a suitable piece of art to put over your mantel, you happened upon and reconnected with an old school pal you hadn't seen in years and whom you didn't even know had moved to your area, or that they were even interested in art!

Or it could have been that while attending a staff party, to which you were literally dragged by your significant other, you met a spouse of one of your mate's coworkers. And after chatting for a while, you discovered that he or she just happened to be looking for an employee to fill a position in their company that fit your career goals, a position that you had been desperately searching for and were beginning to lose hope of ever finding. Then, after a quick resume and short interview, you landed the job of your dreams.

Then again, it could be that while having dinner with friends, you were introduced to a member of the opposite sex who had just arrived from out of town for a visit. It was quite unexpected, but delightful. And thus began a new relationship.

I've had many such surprising encounters in the course of my life, some of them quite delightful and some of them quite painful, if not at least disappointing. Many of the most rewarding surprises are the times when I've been surprised by God.

As I peruse the scriptures, I find that all through the ages, both the Old and New Testaments, God has revealed himself to people of all walks of life in the most surprising ways. Whether it be some Magi from the East following a star that led them to the birthplace of a king, expecting to find him in a royal palace but instead finding him wrapped in cloth in a dusty, smelly manger, or the sons of Jacob looking for food in a foreign land in order to sustain themselves through a severe famine and finding much more than they bargained for. They found the brother they had sold into slavery many years before, now second in command to the Pharaoh and not only able to provide the family with food but more than willing to forgive his brothers for what they had done to him. The Bible is full of surprises like this.

It is my intent to examine some of these biblical surprises, as well as several personal examples from my own life, and then relate what I have learned from these experiences. In so doing, I hope to encourage you in your faith, challenge you to step out and take risks in that same faith, and if possible help you to better recognize the voice of God. So please step back with me into the pages of the Bible and some chapters of my own life, and let me tell you about the God of Surprises.

CHAPTER ONE
Surprised by Freedom

> *"It is for freedom that Christ has set us free. Stand firm, then, and do not let yourselves be burdened again by a yoke of slavery."* (Galatians 5:1)

One early afternoon in February 1975, I was sitting at our kitchen table looking through the Gospels, trying to find a passage I'd read several days before. The passage I was looking for was to be found in the Gospel of Matthew:

> I tell you the truth, if you have faith as small as a mustard seed, you can say to this mountain. "Move from here to there" and it will move. Nothing will be impossible for you. (Matthew 17:20)

I had read that scripture recently in one of the Gospels, but being new to the Bible and new to my faith, for the life of me I didn't quite know where to find it, other than that I knew it was somewhere in one of the Gospels. I was trying to find the scripture because I thought it would somehow help me express my newfound faith and the experience I'd just had regarding that faith.

I had just recently started attending St. Margaret's Community Church in East Vancouver, British Columbia. It was a former Episcopalian Church that was led by Reverend Bob Birch. It was full of life and the Spirit of God. In my short time there, I had heard several people testify to their newfound faith, and each one had quoted a scripture that had some significance to their faith. I was so excited about what I had found that I felt the need to share my faith as well. And if I was going to share, I needed to have a scripture to share; otherwise I might come across as uneducated and silly. (What I really wanted was to come across as knowledgeable and wise, a trait which I now realize resulted from inner pride and self-centeredness.)

After several minutes of searching for this scripture and not being able to find it, I began to get discouraged and was ready to give up. Then I remembered someone saying that if you weren't able to find something, you should pray and ask God to help you find it. With that in mind, I asked God to help me find the scripture I was looking for. I had no sooner uttered those words in my heart than my hand involuntarily turned the pages. I looked down and these words—not from the Gospel of Matthew but from the Gospel of John—stood out before me:

> I tell you the truth, everyone who sins is a slave
> to sin. Now a slave has no permanent place in
> the family, but a son belongs to it forever. So if
> the Son sets you free, you shall be free indeed.
> (John 8:34–36)

I immediately knew why God had led me to that passage. All my adult life, I had been searching for freedom and that is what I had just found: freedom! I had never felt freer in my life. I had been looking for a passage of scripture that would give credence to my newfound faith, but not only did I find such a scripture but God led me to a realization that what I had found was, at long last, the freedom that I had been seeking for most of my life. It was like God had to give me a shake and say, "Wake up, boy, don't you realize what you've just been given?" Talk about surprises. It felt somewhat like a teenager on his eighteenth birthday, unwrapping a small gift from his parents and finding a set of keys... Being somewhat confused as to what he had in his hands, his parents had to lead him out to the garage to show him what the keys represented—a car. And not only a car, but *The Car*, the car he'd always dreamed of owning but never in his wildest imagination ever thought he would have.

As a young man in my late teens and early twenties, I enjoyed going to parties. However, I was not like a lot of people who attended these parties. While they were laughing, chatting, and telling jokes, I was usually found sitting back quietly watching others have fun. I enjoyed watching them, the ease with which they expressed their thoughts and opinions, the joy they seemed to have within them, and the fun they had doing so. But as much as I enjoyed watching them, I yearned for the freedom they had. There were times, of course, when I would try to get things out, but most of the time the words would never get past my lips. My mouth would open to speak, but the words and thoughts that I so desperately wanted to express would just not come. An inner voice would tell me, "People will laugh at you. You will only make yourself look foolish." It felt like my true self was locked inside me, as in a prison, and I was unable to free myself from the bars that held me there. And so, I would settle back in my corner and listen to and enjoy the freedom that, it seemed, everyone else had.

There were times when I was able to find some of the freedom I was looking for. Unfortunately, that tidbit of freedom came through the use of alcohol, and then later drugs like marijuana and hashish. I found that when I had several drinks in me, I was able to overcome some of my inhibitions. Fortunately, through time I also discovered, due to several occasions when I couldn't even remember the previous evening and woke up with a severe hangover, that the alcohol was not really giving me the freedom I was looking for. I came to the realization that the alcohol was actually controlling my behaviour and at times making me look foolish, thus invoking in me the feelings I was desperately trying to avoid. And later, due to a frightening experience I had while on drugs, I decided to give them up as well. Thus, the freedom I was desperately searching for was still lacking and beyond my reach.

That lack of freedom stemmed from my childhood—not that I was brought up in a prison or anything. Nor was I brought up in a home where I didn't have any opportunities to have fun, for having been brought up on the farm in a large family, which included seven boys and five girls, I had plenty of such opportunities. A lot of our fun as children took place in the great outdoors. Whether it was playing Follow the Leader in the tall grass, Hide and Seek in the hayloft, Kick the Can, Cowboys and Indians, or just jumping around in the mud puddles during a summer rain or making mud pies and such, life on the farm was quite often a lot of fun.

I am not saying, though, that our childhood consisted of only play, for there was always an abundance of work to be done on the farm. In our early years it was making beds, cleaning house, weeding in the huge garden next to our home, picking and shelling peas, feeding the chickens, and gathering eggs. As we grew older, for the boys such tasks as feeding the animals, milking cows, cleaning out the barn, working long hours in the fields stacking hay, stooking corn, splitting wood for our furnace, and shovelling grain were added to our list of chores. For the girls, it was cooking, canning, baking, washing and ironing clothes, and washing and drying dishes. In spite of all the hard and tiring work we had to do, I still have fond memories of growing up on the farm.

Looking back, however, there was one thing I really missed—a dad. Not that I didn't have a dad, either; it was just that he wasn't there for me as I believe a real dad should have been. I don't have any memories of spending time with him, or of simple things like being tossed in the air, playing catch, or just sitting on his lap and listening as he explained the facts of life to me.

It's not that he was a complete failure as a father, either. In a lot of ways, he was a good example. He was a hard worker, a good provider, and he established in me and others of the family a solid work ethic. He was friendly and helpful to our neighbours and hospitable to strangers, welcoming them into our home and to the dinner table if they so happened by while we were eating. He was also a man of clean living who had a peace about him most of the time and knew how to have fun. The fun he had, however, seemed mostly to be with other adults, quite often our aunts and uncles. They would sit and play card games like Canasta and Yuker, laughing and drinking tea with home-made bread and jam while those of us still at home played on our own.

There was one distinct thing about his character that I disliked, however, and that also frightened me at times: his Scottish temper, and more importantly his lack of self-control. He could, at times, seem to change instantly and lash out at one of us or one of the animals. I can't really hold that against him, though, as he inherited that temperament from his ancestors and, from what I understand, learned how to express his anger through

their example. Neither, I'm sure, did he have the skilled counsel-
ling available to him as we have today to deal with his temperament and lack of control.

I wasn't all that bothered by his anger towards the animals—or even towards my siblings, though I found it somewhat
frightening. What bothered me the most was when his anger
was directed at me. It often seemed to me that I was being un-
justly punished. There was the time I came home late from
school and was shouted at, followed up by a boot to the back-
side. Even though I had indeed come home late, I might have
been able to justify that anger if my sister, who was just a year-
and-a-half older, had not come home quite some time later
without any punishment being inflicted on her. Neither of us, I
believe, had let our parents know where we were, yet she was
not punished at all. In fact, my father took her on his knees,
hugged her, and smiled at her. I couldn't understand why I got
the brunt of his anger and she didn't. Was it because he disliked
me or even hated me? I often wondered that.

On another occasion, my parents had some relatives over
and they were playing Gin Rummy. My older brother Bill had
taken some rubber rings off the canning jars and was shooting
them at me in the same way you might shoot elastic bands. Of
course, I would pick them up and return fire. After a while, some
of those bands would break from all the stretching they en-
dured. My brother would make a knot in them by tying the ends
together and continue shooting them at me. In response, I
would join right back in and, once again, return fire.

It just happened, though, that on one such occasion my shot hit my brother in the eye. Of course, since it stung immensely, he started to shriek and squeal. All at once, my father got up from the table, walked over to me, and backhanded me across the face. Not only did it hurt physically, but, much worse, it hurt inside. It was my older brother who had started the incident and it was he who had knotted the rubber bands, so why was I getting the hostile treatment just because he happened to be the one to get hit in the eye? Once again, I wondered why my father disliked me so much. What was wrong with me?

It was because of incidents like these and others, and the lack of positive reinforcement in my life, that I started to develop an inferiority complex—not that I understood at the time what that was. I just felt that there was something wrong with me, that I didn't measure up, and that I wasn't loved like my older sister was.

My peers at school, some of them being my cousins, didn't help my situation. There were times when I didn't understand what they were talking about and asked them to explain. Because of my naivety, they often laughed at me and I ended up feeling like a fool. The combination of these putdowns and my father's seemingly unjust anger towards me continued to build in me those inferior feelings, feelings of insignificance and lack of value. Accordingly, I grew up quite withdrawn and shy, wanting but not able to express my true inner feelings for fear that I would be laughed at and made fun of. It was these inner feelings that led to my longing for freedom.

However, as I read the scripture God had led me to in prayer, I realized that I no longer had that overwhelming feeling of insignificance and inferiority. He had set me free. Just the evening before, he had spoken to me in such a manner that I felt, for the first time in my life, that I was very significant and worthwhile. What he said to me that evening I will save for another chapter, but it did, in fact, touch me in such a way that I felt very special. More than that, I was filled with inexpressible joy and a peace that defied explanation. My heart was filled with so much joy that I felt like it was going to burst through my chest, and my feet felt like they were floating two feet off the ground. I felt scrubbed and clean, like a newborn baby. I felt like I had been reborn. Along with all that joy came an acute awareness of my surroundings that I had not observed for years—like the singing of birds, the smell of fresh air, and the beauty of creation. Even the dandelions growing in our yard, the same dandelions I had so desperately tried to eradicate only a few days earlier, looked wonderful to me.

As I look back at that day, I'm reminded of times in my childhood when, in order to escape the pressures and negative feelings in my life, I would find a place of refuge where I could be alone.

In the summertime, I would most often find sanctuary in the tall grass that grew in our yard. When the grass had not been mowed for some time and was midway between my waist and my shoulders (such that I could disappear in it), I would begin to walk through the grass, deliberately making trails in circles that crossed one another. When I thought there were enough crisscrossing trails to sufficiently confuse anyone who might be trying to find me, I would leap off the trail as far as I could possibly go. There, in the tall grass where no trails led and I was all alone, I would lie down on my back and look up at the billowing clouds in the blue sky overhead. In this secret and quiet place of refuge, with no one to disturb me and the wonderful world around me, I would find a place of rest and peace. From that place of rest, I would ponder the sky above and the grass around me, including the insects that crawled through what would seem to them a vast forest of blades of grass, several of them broken by my own weight. In that place of refuge, I sensed a presence that I could not define, a presence I now know to be God.

Freedom is, however, a somewhat elusive thing, and if you are not very careful, you can find yourself entrapped once again in the very same circumstances that you were just released from. Take, for example, an addict who, because of his or her addictions and the crime that arose to feed that addiction, was charged and incarcerated. Upon their release from prison, they have that wonderful sense of being set free. However, if they do not take particular care, they can very easily become ensnared in that same addiction and, in turn, become incarcerated once again.

The same is true of me. Several times the Lord has had to free me from those same old self-images of insignificance and inferiority. I find it is so easy to fall back into the patterns of thought that once controlled my life and held me in bondage.

This is especially true when events in my life go contrary to my desire and I hear a voice saying to me, "You've failed once again. You are a failure." I have come to discover that it is how we perceive ourselves, what we believe about ourselves, that becomes our reality. This is expressed quite clearly in a book I read called *Psycho-Cybernetics,* by Maxwell Maltz, which I will refer to again in the following chapter.[1] This same truth is also implied in the proverb that says, *"For as [a man] thinketh in his heart, so is he"* (Proverbs 23:7, KJV).

Rick Warren, in his book entitled *The Purpose Driven Life,* says, "We are products of our past, but we don't have to be prisoners of it."[2] Though this incorrect perception of myself was something that needed correction and that God had set me free of, there were many other areas of my life where he needed to set me free. Several of those, but not all, had to do with my fears.

Although I did not really think much about it, I had within my being many fears that produced a lot of anxiety. This came to my attention quite remarkably a year or two later in a dream. In my dream, my first wife came to me in our living room and told me that God had revealed to her ten dark things about my life. I asked her to tell me what they were, but she said she was not allowed to. Because I desperately wanted to know, I became quite agitated when she refused and began shouting and demanding that she tell me. It was at this point of the dream, when I was filled with anxiety and rage, that I suddenly awoke.

---

[1] Maltz, Maxwell. *Psycho-Cybernetics* (New York, NY: Pocket Books, 1969).
[2] Warren, Rick. *The Purpose Driven Life* (Grand Rapids, MI: Zondervan, 2002), p. 28.

I lay there wondering what this dream was all about, and as I looked into the darkness searching for meaning, a vision appeared to me of a flower vase, sort of floating in space. I was distinctly aware that this vase represented myself, and as I began to look closer at it I noticed faint lines running all through it like cracks. As I focused more on the cracked vase and what that meant in relation to me, I began to see a thin film surrounding it that was keeping the vase from falling into pieces. God was showing me that I was on the verge of a complete breakdown.

As soon as that realization came to me, however, it was like someone pulled plugs from the ends of my big toes and all my pent-up emotion and tension went swirling out the holes like air being released from a balloon. It was so dramatic that I could physically feel it both in my toes and in my being as the tension just disappeared. I lay there relieved, but at the same time somewhat bewildered as to what this all meant. However, because of the supernatural release of tension, I knew that God was present and in control, and with the anxieties gone I was able to fall back into a deep and peaceful sleep.

Several days or weeks later (I cannot remember exactly how long it was), I was driving my bus back to the bus depot in Burnaby at the end of my day. I had been working for B.C. Hydro as a transit operator in Greater Vancouver for approximately three years. It had been a busy but uneventful day and I was at peace with God and myself. Unexpectedly, God's Spirit spoke to me in that quiet, still voice in which he is most accustomed to speaking. He said, *"Allan, I want you to let go of all your fears."* I was both surprised and somewhat bewildered by this statement, as I hadn't really thought much about my fears. I started to wonder what fears he was referring to. However, as I began to search my inner being, thinking back through my memories, I became aware of several fears that I had.

I was afraid of water, especially the fear of drowning. This fear kept me from going into water where I couldn't see the bottom or where I didn't have something secure to hold on to. If I got into water that was deeper than what I was comfortable with, I would panic and start thrashing about.

I was afraid of bees, so much so that if one flew near me when I was outside mowing the lawn I would quite often flee to the house for protection, leaving the electric mower running in the yard. You can only imagine the embarrassment I felt when, as a man and father of two children, the neighbours observed me doing this.

I was afraid of speaking in public, even to a small group of friends, and so I continued to be that quiet man sitting in the corner where I would be protected from the envisioned laughter and derision of those I was in the company of.

I was afraid of trying new ventures, even simple home projects, for fear of failing. Once again, I suspect, this stemmed from the notion that I might be derided or made fun of by someone.

I was afraid of the dark, especially the darkness of a basement, to the extent that when I went downstairs in my own home at night, I would be constantly looking over my shoulders and feeling the need to run back up the stairs for fear that something or someone would catch me before I made it to the top. That fear, I suspect, came from childhood taunts of the boogeyman hiding downstairs, in the closet, or under the bed.

The late Selwyn Hughes, in his devotional *Every Day with Jesus*, quotes Dr. E. Stanley Jones in regards to fear, who says:

> Fear is the Fifth Columnist within the soul, the Trojan horse that looses from within itself the enemies that capture us within before the real fight with the outward enemy begins.[3]

Shortly after I had identified these fears, I came across a book—the title is beyond my recollection—that spoke of overcoming fears. The main thing I remember about that book was the direct implication that in order to overcome one's fears, one had to face them. That thought was further reinforced by an object lesson I had with our oldest son, Raymond. He had stayed home from school one day complaining of a sore stomach. After some time, I became aware of the fact that he had a part in a school play and there was a rehearsal that afternoon. Putting two and two together, I began to realize that the stomach-ache was most likely "butterflies" due to the fact that, being a lot like me, he was afraid to speak in public. As I realized this, I was reminded of a Sunday school lesson he had brought home recently that dealt with a young boy facing his fears. I found the

---

[3] Hughes, Selwyn. *Every Day with Jesus* (Farnham, UK: CWR, 2009), entry for July 26.

article and read it to him, reflecting on the fact that once the boy in question faced his fear, which was a bully that was tormenting his sister, the bully then backed off. He, in turn, became a hero in the eyes of his sister.

With that reassurance, I was able to persuade my son to go to school. A few days later, his mother and I attended the play that he took part in, and to our delighted surprise, he not only took part in the play but recited his lines with perfect clarity and boldness.

So it was, armed with this newfound discovery and knowing that God was with me, that I decided to begin to face my own fears.

One of the first fears I began to tackle was the fear of speaking in public. That opportunity arose unexpectedly though a member of the church we attended, someone who also happened to be a neighbour. He invited me to attend a service with him at the Union Gospel Mission in downtown Eastside Vancouver.

UGM, as it has become known to me, is a mission in the inner city that has an outreach aimed at the lost and homeless in the vicinity, many of whom have drug and alcohol addictions. Each evening the mission fed approximately one hundred men and women who lined up at their door. A prerequisite for eating, however, was having to sit through a service put on by members of different church congregations in the greater Vancouver area.

So it was that, with my neighbour Doug, I attended a service, not knowing what to expect. Although I just sat, listened, and watched, I felt compassion for those who attended and longed to be able to give them hope.

After my first visit, and due to the fact that I had shared my testimony with Doug, he asked me if I would be willing to share that testimony with the men and women at UGM. Although I was terrified of speaking in public, having been inspired to face my fears and having within me the deep desire to share the good news Gospel of Jesus Christ, I agreed to do so.

On the way there one month later, I was feeling fairly confident that I would be able to carry it off without much difficulty, despite the fact that I was somewhat anxious. However, when I got up on the stage and began to speak, I became absolutely overcome with anxiety. My fear was so intense that I was almost unable to speak at all. I shook physically and lost my train of thought. My anxiety was so intense that my mouth became extremely dry, to the point that words were difficult to form. Such was my fear that at the end of my talk I could not recall most of what I had said.

I felt completely humiliated and, if it had not been for Doug's encouragement, I doubt I ever would have had the courage to do the same again. But because of that encouragement, coupled once again with my desire to share the Gospel and to face and overcome my fears, I continued to take the challenge over the next several months. And as I did so, my fear gradually began to subside. Little by little, I became much less shaky and more able to maintain my train of thought and articulate what it was that I wanted to communicate.

So it was that, with God's help, I gradually faced my fears and overcame them. In the basement, knowing God's promise that he was always with me, I determined to walk slowly up the stairs and not look over my shoulder, trusting that he would protect me. After several occasions of doing this and nothing unusual happening, my fear of the dark—and more importantly, my fear of the basement—gradually began to subside. I can say that I am able to wander around the house in the dark and in other's basements (as I no longer have a basement) without fear and the need to run or look over my shoulder.

One by one, I faced my fears and gradually overcame them. I read and memorized several verses that applied to fear and used them to build confidence in God:

> For you did not receive a spirit that makes you a slave again to fear, but you received the Spirit of sonship. And by him we cry, "Abba, Father." (Romans 8:15)

> For God did not give us a spirit of timidity [fear], but a spirit of power, of love and of self-discipline. (2 Timothy 1:7)

> Cast all your anxiety [fears] on him because he cares for you. (1 Peter 5:7)

> So we say with confidence, 'The Lord is my helper; I will not be afraid. What can man do to me? (Hebrews 13:6)

> There is no fear in love. But perfect love drives
> out fear, because fear has to do with punish-
> ment. The one who fears is not made perfect in
> love. (1 John 4:18)

As the truth of God's Word penetrated my heart and mind, I gradually became less and less fearful, knowing that he is always there for me and watches over me to protect me, working all things together for my good, even the difficult and painful things in my life.

Although there are times in my life when fear strikes me, when I turn to God he reminds me of his love and his promises for me. Because of his reassurance, I have begun to feel somewhat like David, who wrote:

> But I have stilled and quieted my soul; like a
> weaned child with its mother, like a weaned
> child is my soul within me. (Psalms 131:2)

A weaned child is a child who has, first of all, been birthed by its mother. It is a child that has been nurtured, loved, and protected by its mother, both within the womb and after it has been born. It is a child who has felt security in its mother's arms. It is a child who has now been weaned and is no longer feeding at its mother's breasts, but because of the love, protection, and nurture it has received, it feels safe and secure holding its mother's hand as it toddles along. Such a child, when fearful things present themselves, clings to its mother and finds there the security it desires.

So it is with me. When situations arise in my life that cause anxiety or fear, I turn to God. As I do, he reminds me of his promises of faithfulness and love, and his ability to protect me and to work all things together for my good. With that assurance, I find my soul quieted within me and I am able to face those same situations knowing that God is there for me.

CHAPTER TWO
Surprised by Truth

*"You will know the truth, and the truth
will set you free."* (John 8:32)

Truth! What is truth? There are varying opinions on this, but the Oxford Dictionary defines the word "true," the derivative of truth, as, "In accordance with fact or reality, genuine, not spurious or counterfeit."[4] Though some may dispute this, the average person knows some things to be true. For example, we know that birds can fly and bees can sting. We know that hunger is a signal that our body is lacking the nutrients it needs to sustain our organs and muscles. We know that thirst is an indication that we are lacking the liquid our body needs to maintain its natural functions. We know that

[4] Concise Oxford Dictionary, The Ninth Edition (Oxford, NT: Clarendon, 1995), p. 1497.

the force of gravity keeps us from floating into space, that fire burns, and that water freezes if lowered to a certain temperature. These are just a fraction of the many things we know to be true.

There are a lot of things, however, that are not so obvious and that the average person in our society may not agree with. For example, are there certain moral codes that we should follow, or are we free to decide for ourselves what is right and wrong? Are there basic principles which we should live by? Is there a God, or is he just a figment of our imagination? Are we created beings, or did we just evolve by accident or chance? Is our future determined by ourselves, or is it just fate that determines it?

These and many more questions face a large proportion of our society today, especially the younger generation. These are some of the questions I faced personally as a young man. As I mentioned in the previous chapter, I was, for the most part, very quiet and withdrawn. I did not ask a lot of the questions that burned within me for fear of being laughed at. Nonetheless, I still had those questions. I listened to others' thoughts on these and many more issues, and as I listened I heard various opinions. Some opinions were stated as fact, as if there were no other options and the speaker was the official authority on the issue; others were stated as opinions only; and still others were presented as more of a question than an opinion.

The more I listened, the more confused I became as to what was right, since there were strong opinions on both sides of the issues being discussed—and sometimes vehemently debated.

Deep down, I wanted to know the truth, but what was the truth? What was life all about? How was I to live life? What was right and wrong? Why was I feeling so trapped? What could I do to change things? Thus, my quest for truth became as deep as my longing for freedom. In that quest, I began to read books I had heard talked about, which I thought might reveal to me some of the truths I was searching for.

I read books on Zen Buddhism and other schools of thought. As I read these books, I was not convinced that the principles they proclaimed or suggested were, in fact, truth.

There was one book recommended to me, however, that did speak to me as truth. That book was called *Psycho-Cybernetics*, written by Maxwell Maltz, a plastic surgeon. In his book, Maltz reveals how people are affected by their own self-image and how they can change that image by believing and speaking truths about themselves. He uses an example of an attractive young lady who imagines herself to be ugly. Such a woman will act according to what she imagines to be true about herself, and in so doing she will effect the course of her life.[5]

As I read on, one thing I was quite surprised to discover was that I was responsible for my actions, and thus the course of my life. Although I was looking for truth, the truth I discovered here was not only surprising but quite awakening. Up until I read *Psycho-Cybernetics*, I had always believed that I was a victim of the circumstances and injustices in my life. According to my recollection, I saw that to be especially true in regards to my

---

[5] Maltz, Maxwell. *Psycho-Cybernetics* (New York, NY: Pocket Books, 1969), pp. 7-8.

marriage. I knew that Cathy, my first wife, was a major force in our staying together as a couple for so long. She had pursued me and had been the predominant instigator in our sexual relationship as well—not that I was innocent or hadn't been a willing participant. I was aware, though, that because of her desire for children, she had gone out of her way to become pregnant. Once she had become pregnant, she became very possessive and sometimes angry if I so much as looked at another woman.

Cathy and I had been living together for some time and things seemed to be going smoothly until this started. Now, in her fits of anger, she would throw dishes and other household items at me. Due to my immaturity at the time, however, I was not able to understand her anger or the insecurities she was dealing with. I was not able to comprehend how her deep longing to belong and to be part of a happy family was threatened so much by my simple act of admiring another human being. I did not understand the fear she nursed of being left alone with this child growing within her that she so desperately wanted, let alone the embarrassment she would feel in regards to her family and friends if that happened.

What I need to point out is that she had come from a very dysfunctional family. Her father, who was a rather copious indulger of alcohol was, between work, soccer, and the bars, away from home a lot of the time. When he was home, he would often be defending himself from her mother's tirades against his drinking habits or, in his drunken state, disciplining his oldest daughter. She told me of her 8:00 p.m. curfew as a teenager and how, if she was even as much as one minute late, she would be disciplined severely by her father. To escape that heavy discipline, Cathy had run away from home. In due time, she ended up in foster care. During her stay at the foster home, enjoying more freedom and the attention she got from the opposite sex, she fell prey at one point to a young man who took advantage of her youth and insecurities. She had been raped by him and forced, by way of threats, to do things she did not desire to do or feel comfortable doing.

It was after going through this rocky and troublesome time as a youth that she met me. Desiring a stable and non-abusive relationship, she noticed me one evening as I was leaving the rooming house that we both shared. She took a liking to me and endeavoured to pursue a relationship. After getting to know her a little bit, I asked her to dinner with myself and some friends. On our return home, she invited me into her room. It was there that I had my first sexual encounter. And so it was that our relationship began in the northern community of Prince Rupert, where we had both gone to work.

Both of us, being very insecure, immature, and having developed a liking for one another, began to cling to each other. After some time, we rented an apartment together, which we shared with a multitude of cockroaches. However, after some months, due to the type of work I was involved in and the effect it was beginning to have on our relationship, Cathy decided to move back to the lower mainland and take up residence with the foster family she had once lived with.

After a combination of my missing her and my desire to get free of the work I was involved in, I decided to move down to Vancouver, the city I had always longed to go to. I took up residence in Burnaby and there got in touch with Cathy once again. We began to date and she introduced me to her family and friends. We eventually decided to get a place together and moved into a one-bedroom suite in a home in New Westminster.

As much as I enjoyed her companionship and our sexual relationship, I was in no way ready to make a commitment or start a family. So when the fits of anger began, I backed off and moved out to a place of my own. This only troubled her all the more and threatened the secure life she had dreamed of. With her life falling apart, she begged me to marry her, if only to give a name to the child she was bearing within her. When I didn't respond favourably, she attempted to take her life, ending up in the hospital where her stomach was pumped to remove the bottle of painkillers she had taken. I felt tremendous pressure. I wanted to do the right thing. I did not want to be responsible for someone else's life, and yet I did not in any way feel ready or equipped to raise a family. I was being torn apart within and did not know the right thing to do.

After some time, I sought the advice of one of her father's drinking buddies. Being a close friend of the family and desiring the best for her, he advised me to marry Cathy, not knowing all the details of our situation. Without knowing what else to do, and with the pressure of another possible suicide attempt weighing on my shoulders, I agreed to the marriage. As naive as I was, I only married her to give a name to the child and did not in any way understand the implications this would have on our life together.

Of course, Cathy was thrilled, and along with her mother she planned a fairly large wedding. My mother and one of my brothers came out from Manitoba, as well as a good friend whom I'd known from high school and his wife from Calgary, Alberta. The wedding went well in most respects. Cathy looked gorgeous in her wedding gown, and the facilities and food were great. The reception went off without a hitch and everyone seemed to have a great time. To me, however, the whole process seemed like a drill of some kind in which I was just an unknowing participant, not really understanding what was happening but just following along. Even the wedding ceremony felt like a mere procedure. I did not really want to be there, nor did I understand all that was taking place. The vows I made were not really vows but rote, repeating what was said by the presiding pastor. When the reception was over, our honeymoon consisted of a night's stay at a local hotel.

The married life that followed was at first quite similar to the life we'd had previously. It wasn't until our first child was born, a healthy eight-pound boy, that things started to change. I had no real idea of how to be a father, and I felt clumsy in the role. I had no patience with our son and was, in some ways, rather cruel to him. Because he was not always ready to settle down to sleep when putting him to bed or down for a nap, I would sometimes, in my impatience, force his head down onto the pillow. Although I was not intending to be mean, I can see now, looking back, that I was.

Struggling with being a parent and not really being committed to the marriage, I began to spend less and less time at home, preferring to spend it at the bars with Cathy's dad and his friends or with some of my work companions. With the addition of a second son and the added responsibilities that brought, I began to further withdraw from the relationship and spent more time out of the home. Whenever Cathy complained about things, I would quickly respond, "What are you complaining to me for? You got us into this mess in the first place!" To me, that was the reality of the situation and I was quick to blame her for our circumstances.

However, I came to see, through the reading of *Psycho-Cybernetics*, that my circumstances were, in most part, due to the choices I had made in life. For example, I chose to move to Prince Rupert, and I chose to get involved with the type of work I did. I chose to be enticed by Cathy's advances and to accept her invitation to her room. I chose to respond to her seduction and carry on the relationship to the point of living together. After she moved to the lower mainland, I chose to follow her there and renew the relationship. I chose to move in with her once again and continue the sexual relationship. I chose to ignore the implications of that relationship and I chose to leave when her emotional tirades grew worse. When she put pressure on me due to her pregnancy, I chose to seek advice from one of her father's drinking buddies, and also to take that advice. In the end, I chose to agree to her marriage proposal in order to give our child a name. I also chose to spend less time at home and more time at the bar. I chose to throw the blame on her for all our troubles, including finances, although I knew deep down that I was the one who was flittering most of our money away. However, when I came to the realization that most of my problems had a great deal to do with my own choices, I still didn't know how to resolve our problems. Thus, our life together continued much the same as before.

As I mentioned earlier, I had begun to dabble in drugs such as marijuana and hashish. On one of my drinking and smoking evenings with some friends and coworkers, somebody told us about a new movie that had just come out called *Tommy*. He explained that it was a bizarre movie and really quite a "trip," especially if you were stoned. I was intrigued by the movie and desperately wanted to see it while I was high on marijuana. I persuaded Cathy to go with me. Once the film started, I became really caught up in it.

Tommy, a 1974 movie based on the rock opera by The Who, a British rock band, was produced, directed, and distributed by the controversial filmmaker Ken Russell. Starring Anne Margaret, Oliver Reed, The Who, and Peter Townsend, with guest appearances by Tina Turner, Eric Clapton, Elton John, and Jack Nicholson, the movie was about a young boy named Tommy who grew up in a very dysfunctional family somewhat similar to the one I was head of.

As a young boy, Tommy's father got shipped off to war. Soon after, his mother was greeted with the disturbing news that her husband, Tommy's father, was missing in action. In the process of grieving, his mother got involved with another man who came to live with them. One evening, while they were asleep, Tommy's father returned, still in uniform. When he entered the bedroom and discovered another man sleeping with his wife, he became very angry. An argument ensued and the new man pushed Tommy's father, who fell, striking his head on the bedside table. To their horror, the blow took his life. Tommy's stepdad suddenly realized that, as far as anyone knew, the dad was already dead, so if they got rid of the body, no one would know the difference.

The plan was suddenly made more difficult when they saw Tommy, who was awakened by all the commotion, standing in the doorway. The stepdad, in one of the movie's few lines of dialogue, started shouting at Tommy, "You didn't see anything! You didn't hear anything!" From that point on, Tommy was portrayed as blind and deaf, unable to see or hear anything.

As a couple, the parents gave a lot of gifts to Tommy but frequently left him with babysitters who were less than desirable, including a druggie and a homosexual. The one thing they failed to give Tommy was the love and attention he desperately needed. As I watched the film, I became vividly aware of the fact that it was not Tommy who was blind and deaf, but his parents. At the same time, I became aware that, just like Tommy's parents, I too was blind and deaf. I was no different than them. In pursuit of my own happiness, I was not paying attention to or meeting the needs of our children. I was so busy trying to satisfy my own life that I had no time for my family, especially our sons.

I had gone to the movie looking for a thrill, and although I did enjoy the movie, I was totally taken by surprise by the truth that came to me as I watched it. That truth had a tremendous impact on my life and created quite a change in my behaviour. After watching that movie, I immediately gave up my carousing and drinking. I started to do things with the family, especially with the boys. I started taking them swimming and ice skating, although I was hopeless at both. I even began to make an effort in their school work. However, although I tried to be a better parent, I still failed miserably. I just didn't have the skills, freedom, or resources within myself to be an effective parent. I didn't really know how to give them the love they needed. My attempts felt awkward and clumsy.

In spite of the things I'd learned and the changes I'd tried to make in my life, my life had not really changed a great deal overall. There was something, it seemed, that was holding me back, like some unseen force. I began to think it was my marriage. I felt trapped in a marriage that didn't seem to be working. In relation to that, I had purchased a poster that had a picture of a deer and the words, "If you love something, let if go free and if it comes back to you it is yours. If it doesn't, it was never yours in the first place." I hung that poster over our bed, where I hoped it would convey the message to Cathy that I needed to be free, as I didn't really know how to explain to her in a better way what I was searching for. Along with the freedom I desired was a desire for truth. How could I change? What was I doing wrong?

At work, I was getting to know a fellow driver whom I quite admired, George. He always seemed joyful, outgoing, and even caring. As he got to know me, he began to invite me to go to church with him. I turned him down several times, telling him that I would sooner listen to someone on the street than someone behind a pulpit. I didn't really believe in God and didn't trust those who were leaders in the church, especially the Catholic Church. Although that has changed, I perceived, at the time, that the church was interested only in money. I also thought church members were phoney. They appeared to me to put on a totally different appearance on Sundays, even dressing up in their Sunday best, but the rest of the week they were no different than anyone else. George never pressed me, however, but informed me that he would pray for me. I appreciated that, although I had no understanding of the effect of prayer.

Sometime later, I was walking out to the Lougheed Highway to catch a bus home (my car was in the repair shop at the time). Just as I was nearing the highway, my friend George pulled up beside me and asked me where I was going. When I told him my destination, he told me to hop in, as he was going in that direction. As we drove, I must have been telling him some problems I was having with the boys, as I remember his response. He said, "I have five teenage children. Whenever I have a problem with one of them, I find an answer in the book of Proverbs." Because I was looking for answers to my problems, I asked him what the book of Proverbs was. He informed me that it was a book in the Bible.

Upon returning home, I immediately went into our bedroom and reached for the Bible that was sitting atop the headboard. I had been given it by my brother and his wife from Winnipeg on a visit a year or two earlier. At the time, I had indicated to them my interest in the Bible, having just watched the movie *Jesus Christ Superstar*. The next day, after going for a walk to the local mall, they returned with a Bible in hand for me. Due to the genuine interest I had in discovering the truth about the story of Jesus, I began reading it every evening after going to bed.

It brought back memories of the Bible stories I had heard at Vacation Bible School in my younger years. I had attended a weeklong Bible School on two occasions when I was still in grade school. Although I had won a small New Testament for memorizing verses at the time, I hadn't really thought about it since. As I began reading through the books of Genesis and Exodus, I read about Adam and Eve, about Abraham, Isaac and Jacob, about Joseph and Moses, all the familiar stories... but to me, they were still just stories. When I got to the Book of Leviticus, the third book of the Bible, I got bogged down by all the laws of the Old Testament and left the Bible sitting on the headboard of my bed, where it had remained for the last several months.

But now I reached for it, eager to find the book of Proverbs, to get the help George had spoken of regarding his children. By using the table of contents, I found Proverbs, which was written by Solomon, the son of David, king of Israel. Solomon, who is reported to have been a man of great wisdom, wrote the book of Proverbs to reveal truths about life. When I located the book, I did not know these truths. I didn't even find the beginning of the book but instead flipped it open to the third or fourth chapter. I immediately read the first proverb my eyes lit upon. I cannot now recall which one it was, but I do recall that when I read it, it impacted me quite dramatically. It was like a light came on and a simple truth about life, one that I had been searching for, became instantly clear to me.

I was so impressed that I flipped some pages and read another one. Once again, what I read impacted me greatly. An other truth came out of the darkness into the light of my understanding. I was discovering truths about life such as sex, money, and work habits. After the third random reading of these proverbs and the truths that were revealed to me, I began to reflect on the age of the book and that it had been written more than two thousand years in the past. Putting that together with what I'd been taught in school—that our knowledge is increasing as the universe grows older—I wondered how it was that the writer of this book knew more about life than I did, being that I was almost thirty years old and living in the twentieth century.

I also reflected on the fact that the Bible has been called a Holy Book and the Word of God. I began to wonder if there was, in fact, a God, and if this was actually his Word to us. With that thought came also the notion that if this was true, maybe there was a heaven and a hell. Not knowing if any of this was true, but knowing that if it was I definitely knew where I would be going, I started to pray to this unknown God, asking him—if he did, in fact, exist—to forgive me for the way I had been living and to show me how to live.

At that moment, I decided this was definitely the book I needed to read. So I found the beginning of Proverbs and began hungrily reading through the book. When I reached the second chapter, the words I read became alive to me. Not only was I reading them with my eyes, I was hearing them with my ears. Someone was speaking these words to me right there in my bedroom:

> My son, if you accept my words and store up my commands within you, turning your ear to wisdom and applying your heart to understanding, and if you call out for insight and cry aloud for understanding, and if you look for it as for silver and search for it as for hidden treasure, then you will understand the fear of the Lord and find the knowledge of God. For the Lord gives wisdom, and from his mouth come knowledge and understanding. (Proverbs 2:1–6)

With that word, given to me in such a personal way and in answer to my request to him, I tore into the book of Proverbs. Most of it made sense to me, even though some parts I couldn't understand. Nonetheless, my quest for knowledge and wisdom kept me reading whenever I had a chance. I began to take my Bible with me to work, where I would soak up the words of

Proverbs whenever I had time at the end of my bus route. It took me a few days to read through the book, but I finally finished it one Saturday morning.

Because I didn't yet have the seniority to get weekends off, I had begun to work split-shifts on Saturdays, which allowed me to be home during the mornings in order to attend our boys' practises and games, such as soccer and lacrosse. I was driving from 6:00 a.m. until 9:00 a.m., and returning to work from 1:00 p.m. until 6:00 p.m. This allowed me to drive my family to games and practises and also be home for dinner on Saturday evenings.

On this particular Saturday, I finished reading Proverbs and was reflecting on what I had learned—namely, the difference between man's way (the way I and most people I knew were living) and God's way (the way he intended us to live). I was excited about this newfound discovery and couldn't wait to share this news with Cathy. I knew that she had been brought up Catholic by her grandmother in Scotland, and also that she had spoken to me on several occasions about wanting us to take the boys to church. Although I had refused, I thought that because of her background she would be interested in what I had discovered about life and God's Word. So as we sat down to breakfast at the kitchen table, I began, in my own way, to relate to her this pearl of wisdom.

However, my approach to the subject did not exactly go over well. Instead of stating that I was seeing the difference between man's way and God's way, I began by talking about television and newspapers, saying that there wasn't much truth to be found in either and that we should be reading the Bible, where there was much truth to be found. Being that throughout our marriage I had always pushed for my way in a lot of things we shared, and her believing at that moment that what I was trying to tell her was that she shouldn't be watching TV or reading the newspapers, she would have none of it. She immediately cut me off and started talking to the boys as a way to avoid the subject. From my perspective, she had always wanted me to go to church but now that I was interested in spiritual things and wanted to share my discoveries, she didn't want to listen to me. I felt hurt and, in my childish way, started to throw a tantrum. I began banging my fist on the table and shouting, my anger getting the best of me.

I don't know what happened to the time, but all of a sudden I looked at my watch and realized I had only fifteen minutes left to get to work, which was about fifteen minutes away. Not wanting to lose my job and not knowing how to rectify things, I ran out of the house, jumped into my car, and headed off to work. On the way, it became clear to me that I had blown it and made a mess of the morning. I realized that I had not made clear what I had wanted to say and that she had totally misunderstood the message I was trying to relay. I managed to make it to work on time and got behind the driver's seat. However, I felt so bad about what happened that I had trouble greeting my passengers because of the tears in my eyes. I felt desperate and, with tears streaming down my face, I cried out to God in my heart, *Please show her what I was trying to tell her.*

As the day wore on, my feelings of grief and remorse gradually subsided and I began to focus on my passengers. But when my shift ended and I was on my way home, I began to think anew about what I might face when I got there. I wondered if this might be the straw that broke the camel's back. Many possible and depressing scenarios came to me. I pictured my things thrown out on the lawn. I pictured her gone with the boys. I pictured her in distress, having tried to commit suicide again. The best possible scenario I could come up with was an atmosphere in the home that you could "cut with a knife," something I'd experienced several times before in our marriage.

After pulling into our driveway and parking in our carport, I approached the back door apprehensively. The moment I opened the door, however, I saw that things had changed. I stopped suddenly, wondering what was going on. The atmosphere was not at all what I had expected. Instead, it was very pleasant. There was soothing music playing on the radio and the smell of a roast cooking in the oven. My mind immediately went back to the street in front of our home, and I tried to remember if there had been a vehicle parked out front. Maybe we had company, which might explain the bewildering atmosphere. Not being able to recall any parked cars, I gingerly, but quite curiously, went up the three stairs that led to the entrance of our kitchen. As I peered around the corner into the kitchen, Cathy was in the process of setting the table for dinner. Surprised, I couldn't wait to find out what was going on.

As she turned around and saw me, her face beaming like a newly wedded bride, she couldn't wait to tell me what had happened. She began to relay to me the events that happened after I had left the house. She had been in the bedroom crying when it dawned on her that our oldest son, Raymond, had his first lacrosse practise that morning, the practise that I was to have driven them to before returning to work. Being that it was his first practise, she didn't want him to miss it. Realizing the time, and that the practise was going to begin at any moment, she knew that if she was to take the bus, the practise would be over by the time they got there, as both the ride and the practise were an hour long.

Not having a driver's license or a vehicle, her mind scrambled to find a way to get him there. Suddenly, she thought she had the answer: she would phone a cab. Racing to the Yellow Pages in one of the cupboards, she quickly opened it, looking for cab companies. Not being able to find cabs, she realized that she needed to look under "taxi". With her hand positioned to turn the pages to the T's, a number on the page she was on blew up in front of her like someone had put a magnifying glass over it. At the same time, an inner voice told her to phone the number that was magnified in front of her. She told me she argued with the voice, saying she wanted to phone a taxi. But the voice persisted, so she looked to see what the number was listed as.

She was in the C's under churches and the particular number she was looking at was displayed as "Dial-a-Thought." Now she was curious, so she decided to dial the number. After three or four rings, a recorded voice came on the line with a thought for the day. That day's thought was about the difference between man's way and God's way. As soon as she heard the short message, she realized that this was exactly what I had been trying to tell her. She was beaming because God had given her a message to explain my own failed message.

As I heard her explanation of events, I became inwardly ecstatic. I could scarcely believe what she had just told me. What she had just related proved to me that God had miraculously answered my heartfelt prayer. I had asked God to please show her what I was trying to tell her. He had led her to the phone book with the thought of phoning a cab, and before she could turn the pages to the T's, he had magnified the number he wanted her to call and told her to phone it, as the message on the line did, in fact, reveal to her what I had been trying to say.

Up until that moment, I felt there had to be a God, but now I was totally convinced and surprised by the truth that not only was there a God but he heard my prayers and cared enough to answer them, even in a most miraculous way.

Over the thirty-plus years since I came to know God, he has revealed truths to me about life and about myself, and he continues to do so, often in the most surprising ways.

CHAPTER THREE
Surprised by Love

"For God so loved the world [you and I]
that he gave his one and only Son [Jesus
Christ], that whoever believes in him shall
not perish but have eternal life."
(John 3:16)

L ove can be described in many ways, such as an intense feeling of deep fondness or affection for someone—or for something, for that matter. We say to our spouse, our partner, or our children, "I love you." But we also say things like, "I love chocolate," or "I love to sing," or "I love to dance," or "I love to play hockey." Our use of the word love is hugely diverse and very loosely defined.

I appreciate the Greek language and its variations of the word. They have three words for love, each having its own meaning. *Phylio* implies a mutual liking for something, whether it is physical or intellectual. It has to do with comradeship or friendship. From that word, we derive the word "philosophical." *Eros* has to do with sexual intimacy, from which we derive the word "erotic." *Agape* implies devotion, compassion, concern, action, empathy, etc. *Agape* describes the kind of love a parent might have for his or her offspring. It has to do with a person's willingness to go to great lengths for someone to assist, protect, or encourage them, as an individual might endanger themselves or even sacrifice their life in order to save one who is helplessly struggling to survive in a raging river.

Paul, in his attempt to describe that love, writes:

> Love is patient, love is kind. It does not envy, it does not boast, it is not proud. It is not rude, it is not self-seeking, it is not easily angered, it keeps no record of wrongs. Love does not delight in evil but rejoices with the truth. It always protects, always trusts, always hopes, and always perseveres. (1 Corinthians 13:4–7)

It is this type of love that I am writing about and, though I wasn't aware of it at the time, I was searching for it throughout my life. It has to do with accepting another, being there for another in spite of who they are or what they've done. It has to do with encouragement, with fondness and affection. As the above scripture implies, it has to do also with patience, tolerance, trust, protection, and quite often sacrifice.

I experienced a great deal of that kind of love from my mother. She was most always patient and kind with me. She wasn't easily angered, nor, as far as I know, did she keep a score of wrongs. Only once do I remember her being upset with me. That occurred when I falsely accused her of lying to me. She was protective of me, as she was of her other children, and she trusted me to do the right thing. She taught me the importance of earning trust. She never gave up on me and persevered in prayer for me, a fact I didn't know about until several years later. Some of my fondest memories of her love were the times when I was sick in bed with a fever. She would sit by my side and tenderly bathe my forehead with a cool damp facecloth. I loved that affection and the compassion I saw in her eyes as I lay burning up with fever. So much so, in fact, that I almost loved—or should I say, enjoyed—being sick.

I did not feel or see that same love from my father. I cannot recall him showing me any affection. He was often easily angered, and when he was, he did not show patience or kindness, but rather hostility and abrasiveness. I always felt like I didn't measure up and was usually terrified in anticipation of his next outburst. I felt that he disliked me or hated me rather than loved me. I am not saying, however, that he did not love me. I'm only saying that he didn't express his love to me in a way that I could understand.

Gary Chapman, in his book *The Five Love Languages*, explains five fundamental ways of expressing love.[6] They are:

1. Affirmation
2. Quality Time
3. Giving or Receiving Gifts
4. Acts of Service
5. Physical Touch

The book is designed for couples and is meant to help couples discover the language in which their spouse gives and receives love. With this knowledge, it is possible to love your spouse in their own language so that they can understand your love for them. It can, however, be applied in other situations as well.

As I look back on my childhood now, I can see that my dad did love me. His prominent love language was Acts of Service, followed by Gifts. His way of loving me and my siblings was to work hard to provide for our daily needs. Although we didn't have much, we never went without the basic necessities of life. We always had a roof over our heads, plenty to eat and drink, and clothes to wear, even though quite often they were hand-me-downs. He would often, after a hard day's work, be found making treats for us like ice cream, taffy, fudge, or chocolate puffed wheat squares.

---

[6] Chapman, Gary. *The Five Love Languages* (Chicago, IL: Northfield Publishing, 1995).

One of the gifts he provided, if we chose to receive it, was the gift of education. Any one of us who wanted to attend high school and further our education could do so. He paid for room and board in the nearest town, Portage la Prairie, and then supplemented that gift with a small allowance each week for spending money. For someone who didn't have a lot of resources and had a large family to provide for, this act of love, I can see now, was fairly costly to him.

The love languages that I needed as a child, and which I now see every child needs, were Affirmation, Quality Time, and Physical Touch. As I've already expressed, I did not receive those kinds of love from my dad. I do not recall him ever giving me affirmation or spending quality time with me. As for Physical Touch, the times I remember him touching me were far from loving.

So it was that I inwardly searched for love. In my search, I experienced some of that love from Cathy. That was what, in large part, attracted me to her. However, as she became increasingly possessive and manipulative towards me, I started to withdraw. And in spite of the fact that I married her and spent the next several years raising our family and maintaining a home together, I did not really love her much until God began a deep work in my heart, which I will relate in a later chapter.

However, as I began to get to know God through the Bible and answered prayer, I also began to see his love for me as an individual. The first love language he loved me with was Quality Time. That was revealed to me in the way he spoke to me in the

book of Proverbs, explaining to me the facts of life and giving
me guidance, something I cannot recall my dad ever doing.

The second love language he loved me with was Acts of Service. This was portrayed through his giving me an answer to my
first request, as mentioned in the previous chapter. I asked him
to show Cathy what I was trying to tell her and he did exactly
that and even did so instantly, in spite of the fact that I most certainly did not deserve it.

In so doing, God also displayed the language of Affirmation,
in that he was affirming me in regards to the message I was trying to relate to Cathy, letting us both know that what I was trying to express was a positive thing. He was affirming my intentions and not my actions. In spite of the fact that I had completely blown it, God's response was totally different from what
my dad's would have been. I am certain I would have received,
at the very least, an intense scolding for my behaviour from him.

The language of Gift Giving is one of his best, in my opinion, although he is perfect in all languages of love. That gift was
best demonstrated to me shortly after my experience of answered prayer.

After I became convinced that God was real, that his Word
was truth, that he was able to miraculously answer my prayers,
and that he assuredly cared for me, I decided to take George up
on his invitation to go with him to church. As mentioned earlier,
that church was St. Margaret's and was located in East Vancouver. The church was very lively and was pastored by Robert
Birch, a former Episcopalian who was now just a lover of God,

his Word, and his people. It had become very popular, due in part to his acceptance of the "hippies" in the church and, to a large degree, the movement of the Holy Spirit. So much so, in fact, that the building was "bursting at the seams." Every area of the church was occupied by parishioners, including the choir loft and the basement. Because of the crowd and the lack of space, they televised the service and played it live in the basement, where a hundred or so chairs were set up.

I attended the church for the first time with George and was so totally surprised and endeared by it that I persuaded Cathy to come the following Sunday with our sons. Thankfully, she liked the service and the atmosphere, as did our sons, who attended Sunday school. The people were so friendly, hugging and greeting one another, the messages so inspiring, and the music so uplifting that we began attending regularly. As we did, I began to hear the Gospel preached and the message of Christ as portrayed in the Gospels.

I had been given my first Bible due to my expression of interest in the story of Jesus. It wasn't, however, until we started attending St. Margaret's that I began to hear about Jesus in the sermons and learned that the stories of him were recorded in the New Testament, which was the second part of the Bible. And so it was that I began to read the four Gospels and learn about this man named Jesus, who the Bible claims to be both the son of Mary and the son of God. The more I read, the more I came to admire and respect the person Jesus was. I learned about his birth, his baptism, his miracles, his teaching, and most impor-

tantly his love. Here was a man who reached out to the needy
and the lost with compassion and healing. Here was a man who
was respected and followed by the masses. Here also was a man
who loved and spent time with his father in heaven and was willing to do all that he asked of him, even dying on a cross. I began
to love this man, and when I read about his crucifixion I was
deeply saddened.

During this time, I began attending a Bible study at
George's home. Besides him and myself, the only others at the
Bible study were his five teenage children and some of their
friends. Although I was still shy and said little, I really enjoyed
listening to George teach from the scriptures, as well as the
teenagers singing to God in praise and worship and praying for
one another.

On one such evening, George was speaking about the love
of God. Although I had heard about God's love at other times
and was aware that Jesus had died for our sins, George brought
home to me—and others, I'm sure—God's personal love in a
way I had never perceived it in the past. He said, in his own
words, "If you [singular] were the only person on earth, Jesus
would still have come and died on the cross for you." I mar-
velled at that thought and pondered it all the way home and
throughout the evening. I was still pondering it as I lay in my
bed and drifted off to sleep.

When I awoke the next morning, the thought had still not
left me. It had permeated my being with the realization that Jesus Christ had indeed died on the cross for me, Allan Moffat, in

order to pay the penalty of my sins. I was so moved by that realization that I turned to Cathy and said to her, with tears running
down my cheeks, "Christ died for me!" I could understand him
dying for others, but for me it seemed so personal. I was so un-
deserving. I had never thought of myself as being of any value.
And so the verse quoted at the beginning of this chapter penetrated my soul:

> For God so loved the world [you and I] that he
> gave his one and only Son [Jesus Christ], that
> whoever [me] believes in him shall not perish
> but have eternal life. (John 3:16)

What a gift! Not only salvation (a pardon for our sins), but
he gave us eternal life, life after death, so that we could be together with God and his family forever.

And here in this present world, we can experience his abid-
ing presence in the person of the Holy Spirit. His precious
promises are revealed in his Word, his compassion and love
demonstrated in affirmation, quality time, the giving of gifts,
acts of service, physical touch, his protection, his guidance, and
his church—the body of Christ. I can say with certainty, "I have
a father who loves me!"

Because of his love for me, I have come to love him. I love to
spend time with him. I love his Word, the Bible. I love his surprises. I love to serve him and I love his family, the church—not
because my love has been perfected by any means, but because
his love is perfect. As scripture says, *"God is love"* (1 John 4:8).

His love is patient. He is definitely patient with me.

His love is kind. He is extremely kind and gracious to me.

He does not envy what I have, for he has given it all to me in the first place.

He does not boast. He doesn't have to; he is all loving, all knowing, and all powerful.

He is not proud, in that he has to think more highly of himself than he is, for he is above all things and all others.

He is not self-seeking but constantly seeking what is best for his creation, especially mankind, including me and you.

He is not easily angered. But because of his patience and love for us, he is affirming and encouraging.

He keeps no record of wrongs. Scripture says, *"As far as the east is from the west, so far has he removed our transgressions from us"* (Psalms 103:12).

He does not delight in evil, but in fact hates evil. (He doesn't hate evildoers, but rather the evil they commit, because that evil affects people he also loves.)

He rejoices with the truth. He is the author of truth.

He always protects. He has protected me at many different times in my life, particularly from myself.

He always trusts. He trusts me with people, with what he has given me, and with carrying out tasks he assigns me.

He always hopes. Even when I fail him, which I do often, he has the ability to see the best in me, because he knows me better than myself.

He always perseveres. He never gives up on me, even when I give up on myself.

What a great and awesome God I've come to know!

CHAPTER FOUR
Surprised by Grace

*"From the fullness of his grace we have all
received one blessing after another."*
(John 1:16)

G race is most often defined as the unmerited favour of
God. I like those words—*unmerited* and *favour*—
especially when they are used together. The idea of
receiving something favourable, something I didn't have to earn,
pleases me. That grace was best demonstrated in the gift of
God's son, Jesus Christ. His laying down his life in order to pay
the penalty for my sins was definitely a gift of grace. When I look
back on my life and some of the things I've done, I know that my
salvation was truly unmerited—and not only my salvation, but
many other things I've received from him come to mind that I
did not deserve. There are the many friends I've acquired since

coming to know him, who are like family to me. There is my wonderful second wife, who he led into my life, which I'll share about later. There is my good health that, when looking back on my past and how I treated my body, I definitely don't deserve, as well as many other things which are too numerous to mention. There were, however, certain times when I felt he gave me things I definitely didn't deserve.

One such time was several months after I came to know the Lord. I was sitting in the driver's seat of my transit vehicle at the corner of Broadway and Kingsway in Vancouver. The traffic had been light that day and I was several minutes ahead of schedule. As I sat there, I just wanted to escape. I was feeling ill at ease inside and did not want to be around people, but by myself in some secluded place where I could pour my heart out before God. I wasn't sure what I needed. I just did not feel right. I was restless within myself. I had lost the peace and joy I had so richly experienced earlier and I desperately wanted it back. Looking around me, all I could see were buildings, cement sidewalks, vehicles, and people, some who were impatiently looking at me from the rear of the bus, wondering why we were just sitting there. I wanted desperately to escape from it all.

In my search for somewhere to find rest for my soul, my eyes happened upon a small shrub growing next to a building opposite the bus stop. I immediately focused on it as a semblance of nature, which I longed for at the time. As I focused on the shrub, I was reminded of a passage of scripture found in the Gospel of John: *"I am the vine; you are the branches. If a man re-*

mains in me and I in him, he will bear much fruit; apart from me you can do nothing" (John 15:5). I was aware that Jesus was referring to himself as the main trunk, or vine, and his people as the branches. As I reflected on that, I became aware of how the branches drew their life from the vine. As I meditated more on the relevance of that scripture, I was reminded of a message our pastor had just recently spoken concerning the fact that God desired for us to enter into his rest.

As I pondered this, I could readily see how the branches on the shrub I observed near me were not struggling, but resting in the vine. I then looked at my watch and realized it was time to carry on my trip. As I started ahead, I said to God in my heart, *I understand how the branches are just resting in the vine and are not struggling at all.* And with my heart yearning for that rest, I continued, *I understand that your desire for me is to find rest in you, but how do I get there?*

Immediately, God surprised me by speaking these words to me in his still small voice: *"Just know that I love you."* This was exactly what I needed to hear and deep down desperately wanted to know. I was asking him for understanding, and was delighted to receive what I needed: the words "I still love you."

"I still love you." Oh how I needed to hear those words, words my earthly father had never, to my recollection, ever spoken to me, words that spoke life into my being once again, life that I had somehow lost along the way. As soon as I heard them, the peace that I had once experienced and longed for so desperately returned with its original force. That peace once again

flooded my soul, the peace that scripture describes as being "beyond understanding." It had somewhat the same effect as if someone had just lifted me from a drowning experience, where I had been struggling to keep my head above water, and placed me safe and secure in the arms of my saviour.

He did not just say, "I love you," but "I *still* love you." After my initial overwhelming sense of peace, I had come to a place where I gradually lost that peace for the simple reason that I had lost the assurance of God's love for me. That assurance was lost because I had begun to focus on my failings and had begun, once again, listening to those haunting thoughts that insisted I was a failure, insignificant, and of no value. Although I had tried hard to do what was right, I had constantly failed, especially in the area of anger control. I would lose my cool so easily and say things I didn't really mean, things I wish I hadn't. And because of social conditioning and my childhood experiences, I started to believe the enemy's lies that God no longer loved me because I was not worthy of that love. I had forgotten or failed to hold onto his words, such as:

> He does not treat us as our sins deserve or repay us according to our iniquities. For as high as the heavens are above the earth, so great is his love for those who fear him. (Psalms 103:10–11)

> For it is by grace you have been saved, through faith—and this not from yourselves, it is the gift of God—not of works, so that no one can boast. (Ephesians 2:8–9)

For I am convinced that neither death nor life,
neither angels nor demons, neither the present
nor the future, nor any powers, neither height
nor depth, nor anything else in all creation, will
be able to separate us from the love of God that
is in Christ Jesus our Lord. (Romans 8:38–39)

Through the years, the Lord has had to teach me over and
over again that his love for me has nothing to do with my per-
formance but everything to do with his grace.

Another of those times came several years later, shortly after
Cathy divorced me. I had gone back to Winnipeg to visit my
family. My visit was not without some trepidation, as I was not
sure how my family would receive me. I was aware that my failed
marriage had a great deal to do with me and my temperament
and I was unsure whether my siblings would look down on me
because of that. My fears, however, were soon relieved as my
family received me lovingly and graciously. I felt totally accepted
by them and had a really great holiday.

As the holiday was nearing its end, I was regretting my return home where I would once again have to face the loneliness
and pain of my divorce. As my flight home was on a Sunday afternoon, I spent Saturday evening with my oldest living brother,
Ted, and his wife Margaret, the same ones who had given me
my first Bible. We had a wonderful dinner together at their
home and a lovely visit before retiring for the evening.

The next morning I awoke fairly early. As I was lying in bed,
I realized that it was Sunday and that my brother and his wife

would probably ask me to attend church with them. I had on at least two previous visits done so. They attended the First Presbyterian Church in central Winnipeg, where they were both elders. On my previous visits, I found the services and the worship quite dry and did not really want to attend that day. However, I considered the fact that if they were staying with me, they would most likely attend my church, so it was the least I could do in consideration of the love and hospitality they had shown me.

I was also very aware that God could speak through any circumstance. So when they asked, I graciously responded, "Yes!" To my surprise, I really enjoyed the worship this time around and readily joined in with others who were praising God with abandon. There were two hymns we sang that I especially enjoyed and had never heard before. The sermon, given by a female pastor whom I had not heard on previous visits, and who was giving her farewell address, was relevant to where I was at the moment. It was quite enjoyable.

When the service was over, my brother informed me that both he and his wife had to attend an elders meeting. He was quite apologetic and let me know that coffee was being served at the rear of the church. I told them not to worry, that I would be fine and have some coffee and reflect on the architecture of the building, with its stained glass windows. So after getting some coffee, I did just that.

Some time later, I returned to a pew and started to reflect on the message I had just heard and how it applied to my life. I no longer remember what that message was, but I do recall how it caused me to reflect on my position in life. I saw myself as being insignificant, just a farm boy with no real education or talents, a failure, with my marriage and family in disarray and nothing significant to show for my life. My home was gone, and I had very little money in the bank.

Suddenly, I was taken by surprise as a scripture reference popped into my mind. It was Ephesians 2:10. Having been surprised by God in a similar manner several times in the past, I was quite sure God had something to say to me. However, I didn't have my Bible with me, so I tried to recall what that scripture said. Unfortunately, I had not memorized much scripture as of yet. I felt disappointed, but then I recalled that some churches left Bibles in the backs of the pews. I did a quick check and, to my relief, there was one nearby. It was a New English version. I removed it and opened it to Ephesians 2:10, which read, paraphrased from memory:

> For I made you what you are, and in your union with Christ Jesus, I have appointed you unto good works, which I have predestined for you to do.

As I read the words, *"I made you what you are,"* my childhood flashed before my eyes, as if I was taken back in time. I saw my parentage and was aware that I had inherited several qualities of character from my father, and his father in return, some of which were not exactly desirable. I was also aware that I had learned certain qualities from my parents, my siblings, and from my peers both in school and our neighbourhood. In effect, I had been conditioned by my circumstances.

What I got out of that brief revelation was that I was not totally to blame for the person I had become. Some of the innate characteristics that I had, God had given me when he formed me in my mother's womb—even though they were contrary to his will, in that they were a result of sin, dating back to the time of Adam and Eve. And he had placed me in a family and community, where I was influenced and conditioned to become the person that I was. He was taking the onus off of me and putting it on himself and on the nature of sin itself. What a relief! I wasn't totally responsible for the way things had turned out. Although I had failed in so many ways, I wasn't being condemned by God, but rather accepted for who I was: someone who had been created by him and who had no control over who his parents were or over the family and neighbourhood in which he grew up. All of these factors reflected the person I came to be. I am so grateful, however, that he is not content to leave me as I am but is continually moulding me into the image and likeness of his son, Jesus. I only wish he would be quicker about it.

There have been many times in my life where I have been touched by God's grace. However, as I peruse the scriptures, both the Old and New Testaments, I find many examples where God, whose character never changes, has shown grace to his people. One such incident took place during his time on earth in the person of his son, Jesus Christ.

At the beginning of John 8, John describes a time when Jesus was teaching at the temple courts. While he was teaching, a woman who had been caught in adultery was brought to him. Let's pick up the story:

> But Jesus went to the Mount of Olives. At dawn he appeared again in the temple courts, where all the people gathered around him, and he sat down to teach them. The teachers of the law and the Pharisees brought in a woman caught in adultery. They made her stand before the group and said to Jesus, "Teacher, this woman was caught in the act of adultery. In the Law Moses commanded us to stone such women. Now what do you say?"
>
> They were using this question as a trap, in order to have a basis for accusing him. But Jesus bent down and started to write on the ground with his finger. When they kept on questioning him, he straightened up and said to them, "If any one of you is without sin, let him be the first to throw a stone at her." Again he stooped down and wrote on the ground.
>
> At this, those who heard began to go away one at a time, the older ones first, until only Jesus was left, with the woman still standing there. Jesus straightened up and asked her, "Woman, where are they? Has no one condemned you?"
>
> "No one, sir," she said.
>
> "Then neither do I condemn you," Jesus declared. "Go now and leave your life of sin." (John 8:1–11)

As the Pharisees said, the Law of Moses indicated that any-one caught in adultery was to be stoned (put to death). And ac-cording to the Law, they were right. The Law showed the sever-ity of the act of adultery. However, as John writes in his gospel, *"For the law was given through Moses; grace and truth came through Jesus Christ"* (John 1:17). And this was that same Jesus who they had brought the woman before. They had seen Jesus earlier and saw how he treated the downcast and believed that somehow he would vindicate this woman. The scripture says, *"They were using this question as a trap, in order to have a basis for accusing him."*

But Jesus, knowing what they were up to, surprised them by his actions. The scripture says, *"But Jesus bent down and started to write on the ground with his finger."* The scripture doesn't de-clare what he wrote, but my guess is he started to write names of people with whom those same Pharisees, who were accusing the woman, had committed adultery or some other sin with. For *"when they kept on questioning him, he straightened up and said to them, 'If any one of you is without sin, let him be the first to throw a stone at her."* Whether he wrote names or not, what he was im-plying was that they, too, were sinners and deserved the same penalty.

The scripture says, *"At this, those who heard began to go away one at a time, the older ones first."* It is my thought that it was the eldest who were made aware of their own sins first and then left, followed by the younger ones as Jesus wrote more names. We don't know what Jesus wrote in the sand, but we do know that each of the Pharisees was made aware of his own sin and therefore did not have the right to judge the adulteress. For Jesus had said during his Sermon on the Mount:

> Do not judge, or you too will be judged. For in the same way you judge others, you will be judged, and with the measure you use, it will be measured to you. (Matthew 7:1–2)

The elders had brought this woman accused of adultery before Jesus to trick him, but Jesus in his wisdom had turned the situation around to the point that they were the ones accused and, in humiliation, they left him alone with the woman. Talk about surprises.

However, it was not only the Pharisees who were surprised, for *"Jesus straightened up and asked her, 'Woman, where are they? Has no one condemned you?'"* When she replied in the negative, he then said, *"Then neither do I condemn you… Go now and leave your life of sin."* Did she deserve to be stoned? Well, yes. According to the Law, if anyone was caught in adultery by two or more witnesses, they were to be stoned. Being a Jew, she would have been aware of the Law, as she would be aware of the fact that she had broken the Law. And surely she would have been aware of others who had been stoned to death for similar acts. So when she was brought before Jesus by the Pharisees, who were known to be fanatical in their keeping of the Law, she must have been overcome with the fear of death. However, what she probably didn't know or anticipate was the grace of Jesus Christ. So when she was told to go free and was not condemned by him, she must have not only been terribly surprised but totally relieved as well.

But Jesus didn't just end with the words, *"Then neither do I condemn you."* He added, *"Go now and leave your life of sin."* He wasn't just interested in forgiveness; he was interested in the person, the woman, and knew that her present lifestyle was not by any means the life she was intended for, for he had come that she might have life and have it more abundantly, free from the tyranny of sin.

There are many more examples of God's grace in the scriptures. However, my purpose is not to expound scripture but to state that the God of the scriptures is no different than the God of today and of my life. He is still the God of grace and surprises.

CHAPTER FIVE

Surprised by Faithfulness

"Let us hold unswervingly to the hope we
profess, for he who promised is faithful"
(Hebrews 10:23)

Faithfulness is described in the Oxford Dictionary as "loyal, trustworthy, constant and true."[7] It implies that if someone is faithful, you can rely on them to keep their word or promise and you can depend on them to follow through on their commitment. It demonstrates a feeling of trust. Trust, however, does not come easy for most of us, especially as adults. By the time we are adults, most of us have been disappointed by others a few times, sometimes by someone with whom we were

---

[7] Concise Oxford Dictionary, The Ninth Edition (Oxford, NT: Clarendon, 1995), p. 485.

very close and in whom we had put a lot of trust. That someone could be a parent, a close friend, or even a significant other.

For me, that lack of trust had built through the years, starting with my father. As a child, I had the inherent trust that my parents were there to look after me and protect me. But that trust started to erode when my father would lash out at me for no evident reason. I developed a discomfort within myself, a cautiousness and fear of my father rather than trust. That lack of trust was enhanced by my friends at school, who laughed at me when I confided in them, and later by others who took advantage of my friendship and loyalty in various ways. It was particularly enhanced by Cathy, who took advantage of me by pressuring me into a marriage that I wasn't ready for by telling me that it was just to give a name to the child she was expecting. But she then expected me to be committed to her in a normal marital relationship. So it was that when I came to know the Lord and his immeasurable love for me, I still had difficulty trusting him, especially when things in my life were not turning out the way I had anticipated.

It was during one of these times in my life, on a summer day about one-and-a-half years after my conversion, that I was walking home with our family's pet dog, Sparky, at my side. I was returning from my regular morning run, a routine which I had started approximately two years previous. Although the sun was out, the sky was bright, and there were only a few white fluffy clouds in the sky, my spirit was enclosed in darkness. My heart was heavy and burdened, my shoulders were slumped, my head was down, and I was questioning why certain events were happening in my life. What I was really saying, although I didn't verbalize it, was, *If in fact you still love me, God, why are you allowing these things to happen?* I was questioning God's faithfulness. I was asking, *Can I really trust you?*

I was seeking understanding, compassion, or maybe even pity, but what I found that morning was a demonstration of God's faithfulness. In the midst of my burdensome pleadings, God's Spirit spoke to me in that still small voice that he so often speaks in. He said, *"Look at the sun."* I immediately lifted my head to see the sun shining out from behind one of the few clouds in the sky. He continued, *"The sun comes up every morning and goes down every evening without fail. Even when it is cloudy, you can know that it is there shining by the awareness of daylight by day and by the brightness of the moon by night. If it ceased to shine, life as you know it would cease to exist."* Then he said what I really needed to hear. He said, *"And I am more faithful than the sun."*

What a burden lifter! What an answer to my questioning heart! What he was implying was, *"I will always be there for you."* Immediately, words of scripture came back to me, such as Hebrews 13:5—*"Never will I leave you; never will I forsake you"*— and Isaiah 54:10—*"Though the mountains be shaken and the hills be removed, yet my unfailing love will not be shaken nor my covenant of peace be removed' says the Lord, who has compassion on you."*

God has brought me back to that morning several times in my life, times when events in my life were trying and even devastating, times when I found it hard, if not impossible, to see God in the situation. However, I am learning that we always need to know—although the clouds of life roll in and appear to snuff out the light to the point where it seems we are walking in darkness—that God's love remains constant and continues to shine on us. Just as the clouds eventually clear and the fullness of the sun shines bright once again, so will those events in our lives that seem to block out the brightness of God's love evaporate and leave us enjoying the fullness of his love once again. Our trials, as clouds, are only temporary.

I could just as easily have included this story in the chapter "Surprised by Love," as this was also a demonstration of God's love for me. Just like Thomas, one of the disciples who doubted Jesus' resurrection from the dead when told by the other disciples that Jesus had appeared to them, I too was in doubt. God had revealed to me in a powerful way that he loved me dearly. And he had spoken to me in his Word that he would never leave me or forsake me, yet because of the circumstances I was going through, I doubted his love for me.

If you read the account of Thomas in John 20, you will note that Jesus did not scold Thomas for his lack of faith, nor did he make fun of him for doubting the resurrection. Rather, Jesus came to him and gave him the assurance that Thomas needed in order to satisfy his doubt. He said, *"Put your finger here; see my hands. Reach out your hand and put it into my side; Stop doubting and believe"* (John 20:27). Thomas's reply was, *"My Lord and my*

God!" (John 20:28) Thomas' doubts had just been completely washed away.

In the same manner that Jesus dealt with Thomas's doubt, he dealt with my doubt. He did not scold me or lash out at me as my father had often done, nor did he make fun of my questioning, as my peers in school had. Rather, he came to me at my point of doubt and revealed to me, in a way that I could understand and appreciate, that his love was indeed faithful, that he was always there for me—that just as the sun was always there giving warmth and life to the planet, even when it was hidden by the darkening clouds, he too was there watching over me in the midst of the darkening storms of life. He is a faithful and loving God. And he is not only there for me; he is there for you also. God is no respecter of persons. He loves each one of us and *"wants all men to be saved and to come to the knowledge of the truth"* (1 Timothy 2:4).

God, speaking through Isaiah the prophet to his people, said:

> Can a mother forget the baby at her breast and
> have no compassion on the child she has borne?
> Thou she may forget, I will not forget you!
> (Isaiah 49:15)

The scriptures speak often about the faithfulness of God, and I, too, can speak volumes about his faithfulness. At the beginning of this chapter, I commented that faithfulness implies that if someone is faithful, you can rely on them to keep their promise. One of Jesus' words given to us, God's children, is *"Ask and it will be given to you; seek and you will find; knock and the door will be opened to you"* (Matthew 7:7). I've asked many things from God over the years, and in his faithfulness he has given me most of what I've asked for.

One such time that God was faithful in keeping his promise came during the first summer after I had come to know him. As a parent who had not been there for my sons much in the past, I had a deep desire to give them the experiences that most boys should enjoy, things they had missed out on, such as fishing. Having done very little fishing myself and not knowing much at all about the subject, I spoke with a good friend of the family who was an avid fisherman, asking him where I might take them fishing. He mentioned a lake, Lightning Lake, in Manning Park, a provincial park in the Rockies. He went on to tell me about some cabins that you could rent there and some of the other attractions in the area. The place sounded ideal, especially the cabins, as Cathy did not at all enjoy tenting. So, in spite of my uncertainties regarding my ability to catch fish, I called Manning Park that spring and booked a cabin for three nights in August, when the boys would be out of school.

It so happened that I had just finished reading a biography of a man in a Florida prison who had become a Christian. This man—I no longer recall his name or the title of the book—was a lawyer who had represented and then become involved with a crime syndicate. He had been convicted and sentenced to fifty years in prison.

While in prison, he cried out to God for help and received the gift of salvation. He became so caught up with the love of God that he began to study the scriptures and eventually became ordained as a pastor. After several years, he was suddenly given clemency and released from prison with more than half his sentence still left unserved.

After having been released, and together with his wife and two young children, they began a journey to take up his first pastoral position in California. They had very little money and an old vehicle, but they were trusting God to get them there safely.

While travelling through a desert region in southern California, they were speaking to the children in the back seat about how God answers prayer. Their daughter, who was quite young, asked if God answered the prayers of children. Her parents assured her that he would. And so with that assurance, she began to pray and ask God for snow, something which she had never experienced before, having grown up in Florida. Her parents, of course, began to wonder how they were going to explain to their daughter why God did not answer her prayers as they were in the California desert in the middle of the summer.

But as they pondered this question, suddenly, to their surprise and amazement, it began to snow. Their children were delighted—not only because it was snowing, but because God had answered her prayer. They were amazed by the sudden snowfall and so were the owners of a small service station where they stopped to fill up their vehicle. The owner was standing outside looking up to the sky with an awed look in his eyes, for in his lifetime he had never before seen snow in the area.

Having been encouraged by this miraculous answer to prayer, and not really knowing much about the area around Lightning Lake, or the aspects of catching fish, I knew that I would need God's help. I asked him for two things that I felt were most important: good weather, and the boys having the opportunity and excitement of catching a fish.

As the time approached for us to travel to Manning Park, however, we were in the midst of an incessant rainy period. Not only was it raining for days on end, but it was a heavy rain. So as we began our journey to our destination, I was again questioning God as to whether he would in fact deliver on his promise to give me what I asked. It continued to rain all the way up to the park and throughout the evening. It was still raining heavily when we arrived at our destination. As quickly as possible, we unpacked and settled into our cabin, which was small but cosy. It had two bedrooms, one of which had bunk beds that the boys were excited about. There was a small but adequate kitchen and a quaint living room with a wood stove and an ample supply of dried wood.

Because of the rainfall and the lack of entertainment, especially in that kind of weather, we found refuge at a nature hut that was close by to our cabin. Here, we explored pictures and explanations of animal life in the area as well as some stuffed species of the same. We watched a film on the area which described the sights to see and the animal life. Before leaving, I spoke with one of the naturalists there, asking him for advice on where to catch fish, still hoping that God would come through on his promise to give me what I had asked of him. He mentioned that a good spot was, in fact, Lightning Lake and that there were boat rentals there. He told me that if I rented a boat and paddled out to the far end of the lake, I would find the stump of a tree that was protruding out of the water, to which I could tie the boat. He said that it would be a good spot to fish from.

After having asked him what kind of bait I should use, he advised me to use a dry shrimp fly. Not having such a fly, I asked him whether there was any place I could get them. He said there was a store up the highway another mile or two where I would most likely be able to find all sorts of baits. Thus, with my family in tow, I proceeded up the highway in the rain and found the store. To my delighted surprise, I was able to purchase two of his recommended flies as well as some snacks for the evening.

When we awoke the next morning and looked out the window, we were greeted by the sight of some deer grazing on the grass outside our cabin and, I must add, still more rain. The rain, however, had lessened to more of a drizzle. After a hearty breakfast and with a somewhat optimistic attitude, I decided to check out this Lightning Lake.

Following the instructions I had been given, and with the boys and our fishing gear in hand, we arrived at the lake and the boathouse I had been told about. With the rain diminished and some blue sky starting to appear through the clouds, I found the

person in charge and inquired of the cost of the boat rental. By
then, the rain had stopped, the clouds were further dissipating,
and the sun was beginning to break through, so I decided to
purchase a rental.

After getting our fishing gear on board and our life jackets
securely fitted, I began to paddle out to the far end of the lake.
As I approached the end, I was delighted to find the stump I had
been told about. After tying up the boat, I began the slow and
tedious task of attaching the flies to the lines in such a manner
that they would not come loose. Having only two rods, I set the
boys up with one apiece. After demonstrating how to cast the
line out, they soon caught on and to their delight began reeling
in some small but edible rainbow trout. Boy, were they excited,
as was I, watching and assisting them. After an hour or two, and
seven or eight trout hanging from a line on the side of the boat,
we finally untied the boat from the stump and started paddling
back to the boathouse.

Not only did the boys catch some fish that afternoon, they
seemed to be the only ones doing so. There hadn't been any
other boats on the water, but there were several people casting
their lines from the shore to no avail. What a celebration we had
that evening as we feasted on fresh pan-fried trout.

The following two days were spent exploring the area, including the Alpine meadows across the highway and up the
mountain near our cabin. The weather remained glorious, so
glorious in fact that one of the naturalists observed that it was
the best weather they'd had all summer.

The following morning when we got up and began to pack, the rain started up once again. But in spite of the dark clouds hanging over my head, my spirit was lifted, for God had just given me the answer to my prayers. He had broken the incumbent weather for the three consecutive days we were there, and not insignificantly, for it was, as the naturalist said, the best weather of the summer. Plus, he had enabled the boys to catch some fish in spite of the fact that others were not able to do so. And in doing so, he had strengthened my faith in him and his ability to answer prayer.

As mentioned earlier, I could speak volumes about God's faithfulness to me in answered prayer and in keeping his promises. I will end, however, with the words from a great old hymn that goes like this:

> Great is thy faithfulness, oh God my father.
> There is no shadow of turning with Thee.
> Thou changeth not, thy compassions, they fail not.
> As thou has been, Thy forever will be.

CHAPTER SIX

Surprised by Conviction

"For the word of God is living and active.
Sharper than any double-edged sword, it
penetrates even to dividing soul and spirit,
joints and marrow; it judges the thoughts
and attitudes of the heart."
(Hebrews 4:12)

The Oxford Concise Dictionary defines conviction as "the act or process of proving or finding guilty."[8] One, however, can be found guilty outwardly, as by a court of law, and yet not be convicted inwardly, as in the case of Clifford Olson, a British Columbia man convicted of mass murder in the 1980s. Although he confessed to these killings and has spent many years since incarcerated in federal prison, I would

---

[8] Ibid., p. 293.

have to surmise he has not been convicted inwardly. He has shown no remorse and still tries to benefit financially, and I would suspect egotistically, from his crimes, by having them written of in book form.

The opposite is also true. One can be convicted inwardly without being convicted outwardly, as, let's say, a child who stole a toy from his neighbour's home and is convicted when he hears how much the loss has affected his friend and decides to return the toy to his neighbour and apologize. Inward conviction brings change to a person's behaviour, an about turn (repentance). Outward conviction may or may not bring about the same change. It is my intention to deal not with outward conviction but inward conviction, and also to convey the truth that God does not change. He is the same yesterday, today, and forever. He is a God not only of conviction, but of surprises!

So please bear with me as we look once again into the pages of scripture and then into the pages of my life.

In 2 Samuel 11, it is recorded how King David, a man chosen and anointed by God to be king over Israel—and whom God refers to as *"a man after my own heart"* (Acts 13:22)—commits sins against one of his soldiers. Let's pick up the story as it unfolds, beginning with the first verse.

> In the spring, at the time when kings go off to war, David sent Joab out with the king's men and the whole Israelite army. They destroyed the Ammonites and besieged Rabbah. But David remained in Jerusalem. (2 Samuel 11:1)

"But David remained in Jerusalem." Why did David remain in Jerusalem when it was the custom in those days for the king to lead the soldiers into battle? Scripture does not explain why David stayed home, but as the rest of the story unfolds, one may easily conclude that David was most likely wrestling with lust and his own self importance, for the story goes on to say:

> One evening David got up from his bed and walked around on the roof of the palace. From the roof he saw a woman bathing. The woman was very beautiful, and David sent someone to find out about her. (2 Samuel 11:2–3)

Again, I ask, why was David walking around on the roof in the middle of the night? And why, when he saw the woman bathing, did he send someone to find out about her? Again, scripture doesn't explain, but knowing my own struggles with lust, I can almost see David getting out of bed and going up on the roof of the palace, pacing around on the roof, trying to deal with the lust that is raging in his body. Then when he sees the woman bathing and her exquisite beauty, as king he has no trouble exercising his authority and having her brought to him.

But David, don't you, a man of God, know better? Surely you must be aware of the tenth commandment:

> You shall not covet your neighbour's house. You shall not covet your neighbour's wife, or his man-servant or maidservant, his ox or donkey, or any-

thing that belongs to your neighbour. (Exodus 20:17)

I'm quite sure he did know better, but my guess is that the lust within him, coupled with Bathsheba's beauty, overpowered his judgment, and when the man said, *"Isn't this Bathsheba, the daughter of Eliam and the wife of Uriah the Hittite?"* (2 Samuel 11:3), it did not deter him whatsoever. Nor was it a match for any moral hesitations he may have had, for he sent messengers to get her. What makes matters even worse is this: not only was she the wife of his neighbour, she was the wife of one of his own soldiers who was out fighting on behalf of his kingdom, where he as their leader should also have been.

Scripture goes on to say, *"She came to him, and he slept with her... Then she went back home"* (2 Samuel 11:4). He slept with her! All that burning passion within him was now satisfied, but at what cost? As I see it, he has just broken another of the commandments: *"You shall not commit adultery"* (Exodus 20:14). The temptation, it seems, was too much for him. Now not only was he guilty of lust, but also adultery. What is happening to you, David?

But I have to ask this question: is David any different from the rest of us? Aren't we all tempted with one thing or another? And haven't we at times, when we let that temptation linger in our minds, been overpowered by it and given in to it? Scripture says, *"Each one is tempted when, by his own evil desire, he is dragged away and enticed"* (James 1:14).

For David, things just go downhill from here. Scripture says, *"The woman conceived and sent word to David, saying, 'I am pregnant'"* (2 Samuel 11:5). Just what David wanted to hear! The "roll in the hay" that satisfied his inner passion has now become a problem. The woman is pregnant. *What should I do?* he must have asked himself. David has a choice to make—*Do I repent, and make amends with Uriah, her husband, or can I find a way to make the matter go away?* The first choice, it seems, is too difficult for David. *What will people think if they find out? What will become of my reputation?* Faced with the foolishness of his ways and the inevitable damage that will be done to his reputation, never mind his pride, he chooses the latter option.

Scripture says:

> So David sent this word to Joab: "Send me Uriah the Hittite." And Joab sent him to David. When Uriah came to him, David asked him how Joab was, how the soldiers were and how the war was going. Then David said to Uriah, "Go down to your house and wash your feet." So Uriah left the palace, and a gift from the king was sent after him. But Uriah slept at the entrance to the palace with all his master's servants and did not go down to his house. (2 Samuel 11:6–9)

Now we see the real reason David had Uriah brought home. He obviously thought that Uriah would go home and sleep with his wife so that when the baby was born, he would think it was his own.

> When David was told, "Uriah did not go home," he
> asked him, "Haven't you just come from a distance?
> Why didn't you go home?"
>
> Uriah said to David, "The ark and Israel and Ju-
> dah are staying in tents, and my master Joab and my
> lord's men are camped in the open fields. How
> could I go to my house to eat and drink and lie with
> my wife? As surely as you live, I will not do such a
> thing!" (2 Samuel 11:10–11)

Aren't you ashamed of yourself, David? Here is one of your
faithful subjects who, because of his loyalty to you and his country, won't even spend the evening with his wife but prefers to
sleep outdoors like his fellow companions. Doesn't this kind of
loyalty have any effect on your heart? Obviously not, for David
now tries to get Uriah drunk, hoping that in his drunken state he
will then sleep with his wife.

> Then David said to him, "Stay here one more day,
> and tomorrow I will send you back." So Uriah re-
> mained in Jerusalem that day and the next. At Da-
> vid's invitation, he ate and drank with him, and Da-
> vid made him drunk. But in the evening Uriah went
> out to sleep on his mat among his master's servants;
> he did not go home. (2 Samuel 11:12–13)

Once again, David's plan has failed, so as a last resort he
takes desperate action. He plots Uriah's death. Scripture says:

In the morning David wrote a letter to Joab and sent it with Uriah. In it he wrote, "Put Uriah in the front line where the fighting is fiercest. Then withdraw from him so he will be struck down and die." (2 Samuel 11:14–15)

What is this, David? To what extent will you go to cover up your sin? Isn't this premeditated murder? Isn't it amazing the extent to which people—even we—will go to in order to cover up a sin? It is like the snowball effect, ever increasing until it finally brings destruction.

Scripture says:

So while Joab had the city under siege, he put Uriah at a place where he knew the strongest defenders were. When the men of the city came out and fought against Joab, some of the men in David's army fell; moreover, Uriah the Hittite died. Joab sent David a full account of the battle. (2 Samuel 11:16–18)

As they say in baseball, "One, two, three strikes, you're out." Way to go, David! Any court of law would have no trouble finding you guilty, with all this evidence stacked against you. Aren't you a fine example of the leader of God's chosen people?

I can only imagine the relief David would have felt at this time. Things finally seem to be working out for him. His plan is succeeding. Now that Uriah is dead, he will be free to take Bathsheba as his wife. When the child is born, no one will be the wiser.

The story continues:

> When Uriah's wife heard that her husband was
> dead, she mourned for him. After the time of
> mourning was over, David had her brought to his
> house, and she became his wife and bore him a son.
> (2 Samuel 11:26–27)

Finally his plan to cover his sin has succeeded, and he can now relax. However, he has forgotten one thing, the most important thing: the Lord is watching over his servant and is fully aware of all that is taking place. He may have deceived his neighbours, but he hasn't deceived God. Scripture says next, *"But the thing David had done displeased the Lord"* (2 Samuel 11:27). Of course it displeased the Lord, for he had broken just about every commandment in the book. He should have known better. After all, he knew the Lord and knew the Law and what God expected of him. But somehow he had digressed to the point where he put himself and his own self-interest ahead of God.

Scripture says, *"The heart is deceitful above all things"* (Jeremiah 17:9). David was certainly being deceitful, trying first to deceive Uriah and then his neighbours and his subjects. But from my perspective, the only one he succeeded in deceiving was himself. Scripture says, *"Your sin will find you out"* (Numbers 32:23). And again, *"Do not be deceived: God cannot be mocked. A*

man reaps what he sows. The one who sows to please his sinful na-
ture, from that nature will reap destruction" (Galatians 6:7–8).
David's sins were about to find him out.

Let's pick up the story once again.

> The Lord sent Nathan to David. When he came to
> him, he said, "There were two men in a certain
> town, one rich and the other poor. The rich man
> had a very large number of cattle and sheep, but the
> poor man had nothing except one little ewe lamb he
> had bought. He raised it, and it grew up with him
> and his children. It shared his food, drank from his
> cup and even slept in his arms. It was like a daughter
> to him. Now a traveler came to the rich man, but the
> rich man refrained from taking one of his own sheep
> or cattle to prepare a meal for the traveler who had
> come to him. Instead, he took the ewe lamb that be-
> longed to the poor man and prepared it for the one
> who had come to him."
>
> David burned with anger [righteous anger]
> against the man and said to Nathan, "As surely as
> the Lord lives, the man who did this deserves to die.
> He must pay for that lamb four times over, because
> he did such a thing and had no pity." (2 Samuel
> 12:1–6)

David had a right to be angry, for what this man had done
was insensitive, self-centered, and downright unjust. David was
overcome with a desire for justice and, in one sense, justice is
what he found. His sin would have consequences. But he had no
idea what was coming next. He was in for a great surprise.

Then Nathan said to David, "You are that man! This is what the Lord, the God of Israel, says: 'I appointed you king over Israel, and I delivered you from the hand of Saul. I gave your master's house to you, and your master's wives into your arms. I gave you the house of Israel and Judah. And if all this had been too little, I would have given you even more. Why did you despise the word of the Lord by doing what is evil in his eyes? You struck down Uriah the Hittite with the sword and took his wife to be your own. You killed him with the sword of the Ammonites. Now, therefore, the sword will never depart from your house, because you despised me and took the wife of Uriah the Hittite to be your own.'" (2 Samuel 12:7–10)

At this point, I believe, David had found more than justice; he had found conviction, an inner conviction that cut to his heart. *"Then David said to Nathan, 'I have sinned against the Lord'"* (2 Samuel 12:13). The depth of his conviction is revealed in one of his psalms, said to have been written when Nathan came to him after he had committed adultery with Bathsheba. In it, he says,

Have mercy on me, O God, according to your unfailing love; according to your great compassion blot out my transgressions. Wash away all my iniquity and cleanse me from my sin. For I know my transgressions, and my sin is always before me. Against you, you only, have I sinned and done what is evil in your sight, so that you are proved right when you speak and justified when you judge. (Psalms 51:1–4)

David, I believe, was a changed man. Not only was his life changed from here on because of the consequences of his sins, as Nathan said—*"Now, therefore, the sword will never depart from your house"*—but because of the word spoken to him by God through the prophet Nathan, he appears to have had a deep inner conviction and repented.

God's Word has a way of cutting right to the heart. He knows exactly what we need to hear and when and how we need to hear it, for he knows us completely. He knows everything about us. Listen to David's words, this time in Psalm 139:

> Oh Lord you have searched me and you know me. You know when I sit and when I rise; you perceive my thoughts from afar. You discern my going out and my lying down; you are familiar with all my ways. Before a word is on my tongue you know it completely, O Lord. (Psalms 139:1–4)

In my own personal life, I have been convicted by God's Spirit many times. Sometimes I have had to be convicted repeatedly for similar offences. Because of our wayward nature and our desire to have our own way and be in charge of our lives, we have a tendency to fall to the same temptations over and over again. We tell ourselves that what we are doing is personal and has no effect on anyone else. I have come to the conclusion, however, that sin is sin, and sin always affects our rela-

tionships, whether it is with our spouse, our family, our neighbours, our employers, or our employees. The list goes on. But
more importantly, it affects our relationship with God himself.

I recall a particular time early in my walk with the Lord
when God convicted me deeply and brought about an instant
and dramatic change in my life. It happened one evening at my
friend George's house—the same man who introduced me to
the book of Proverbs, shared with me the love of God, and introduced me to the church my family and I came to attend.

I had begun to attend a Bible study at his house. It was gen-
erally attended by me, himself, his teenage children, and some of
their friends. Although I was still an introvert, I really enjoyed
being there and being a part (mostly as a listener) of the interac-
tion that was going on. In fact, Cathy encouraged me to go, as
she saw that my time there had a positive influence on me.

On this particular evening, George was sharing something
from his heart concerning scripture. Normally, the young people there were very attentive, just as I was, and would be asking
questions and soaking up what George was sharing. On this particular evening, however, they weren't really paying attention,
and were distracting and acting rather foolish. It was so unlike
them and so disturbing to me that I sort of looked up to question God as to what was going on. What I saw was an apparition
of the devil looking down at us and laughing with glee.

Now I was really disturbed… so much so that I, one who
seldom opened his mouth, spoke up, cutting George off in mid-
sentence. What I observed troubled me so much that I just

couldn't hold it in. As I shared this information with him, the young people started to share similar feelings and that they, too, were uncomfortable with what was happening. On hearing our concerns, George decided to end his talk and pray about our concerns. Thus the evening ended sooner than normal and we began to have tea.

At that time, George's wife Carole came in. She was a nurse and was just arriving home from work. I had never met her before, since she was usually at work during our evenings together and did not arrive home until after I left. I was introduced and began to learn some things about the family that I had not previously known, things that somewhat shocked me. I learned that these were not her children, but rather George's children from a previous marriage. I also learned that George was an alcoholic and that at least one of his children was an alcoholic also. What an eye opener! Up until then, I had pictured them as a perfect family.

The fact that they had shared these private matters with me enabled me to see them as normal, imperfect people who struggled with things in their lives just as I did. In fact, it enabled me, for the first time in my life, to be able to open up and share my failings. I shared with them about my marriage. I shared with them how unfair I had been with my wife, by blaming her for our problems. I shared with them how rotten I was to Cathy. I told them that, whenever she complained to me about our relationship, I would say to her, "What are you complaining to me for? You were the one who got us into this mess in the first place." I had the habit, one I either inherited from my father or at least learned from him, of not admitting when I was wrong. I can remember Cathy saying to me, "You would argue that black is white," and "You're just like your father. He never admits when he's wrong."

Needless to say, I opened up that evening and let these people know some of the real me. I told them some things that I was ashamed of, and yet I felt totally accepted by them. It was absolutely wonderful to begin to show the real me and, more than that, to be accepted as I was—to not be laughed at or scolded but to be accepted for who I was in spite of my failings.

What a totally wonderful feeling I left with that evening. Here were some people that I didn't have to put on a front for, who accepted me for who I was. As I was about to head out the door, I can remember George giving me a big hug and telling me to drive safely. I left with all these unbelievably wonderful feelings flooding over me—feelings of peace, acceptance, freedom, and of being loved. But God had much more for me. I walked out their door and into the parking lot. I got into my 1960s Ford Mercury and started the engine. I put it in reverse and peered back over my right shoulder in order to see behind me in the dark. Just then, someone spoke to me. Not only did the voice speak to me, but it addressed me by name. The voice said, "Allan."

I was taken totally by surprise and was shocked and frightened at the same time. As far as I knew, I was alone in the vehicle, and I immediately froze when I heard my name. I carefully started to check the back seat, unsure of who I'd find, being late at night and all alone, other than the person who had just spoken to me. Then I heard my name once again, only this time I recognized where it was coming from. It was not from the back seat at all, but from heaven.

It was the most powerful and yet most loving voice I'd ever heard. Powerful, in the sense that it was like the rolling of thunder, as scripture says, *"like the sound of rushing waters"* (Revelation 1:15). Loving, in that it was one of the gentlest voices I'd ever heard. Yet, what he said next was direct and penetrating, so penetrating, in fact, that it cut right to the core of my being. What God said to me that evening I will never forget. He said, *"Allan, you told those people in there how rotten you've been to your wife, but you've never told her."* That word entered my heart like a knife. I collapsed in my seat like I had been slain.

The writer of the book of Hebrews describes God's Word this way:

> For the word of God is living and active. Sharper than any double-edged sword, it penetrates even to dividing soul and spirit, joints and marrow; it judges the thoughts and attitudes of the heart. Nothing in all creation is hidden from God's sight. Everything is uncovered and laid bare before the eyes of him to whom we must give account. (Hebrews 4:12–13)

How his words spoke to me! I had walked out of my friend's home that evening feeling quite pleased with myself, even a little smug and possibly even a little self-righteous—like David. But just as God had a surprise for David, he had a surprise for me. Just as he spoke to David a strong word of inner conviction, he did the same to me. Just as he brought David down from his high horse, so to speak, he brought me down into a crumpled ball, sobbing in the driver's seat of my car.

As already mentioned, I was full of all of these wonderful feelings of peace, love, and acceptance as I walked out of my friend's home. I was feeling pretty good about myself, in that I had broken my silence and revealed part of my true self. But God told me what I hadn't done and, far more importantly, what I needed to do. I had taken one step by confessing to my friends how I had treated my wife, but I needed to take a much larger one and confess to her, the one I'd wronged, and admit to her how unfair and rotten I'd been.

As I sat crumpled there in the seat, in tears of conviction, two things happened, one right after the other. The first was the realization that God had spoken to me, this insignificant being, this failure in life. Just as he had spoken to Moses and just as he had spoken to the apostle Paul, he had spoken to me. That realization brought with it a sudden surge of life and a tremendous feeling of significance that was the beginning of the freedom I wrote about earlier. Accompanying these feelings was a strong desire to praise God.

The second thing that happened was a strong desire to confess to my wife how wrong I'd been and to tell her I loved her. With both of these desires almost overwhelming me at the same time, I backed out of my parking spot and, almost fervently, began to head home. I was simultaneously praising God and asking him to give me the courage to make a confession. The following day, as I thought back on the events of the evening, I recalled with humour how George had told me to drive safely, and how I had driven across the Port Mann Bridge totally focused on God, with tears in my eyes praising him and, I'm quite sure, with my hands in the air at times.

Anyhow, I got home safely, and immediately upon entering our house went straight into the bedroom and woke Cathy to tell her I loved her and how terribly wrong I'd been to her. I'll never forget how she looked at me. She seemed as frightened as she would be with a complete stranger. For, in fact, I would have appeared to her as a stranger, as my actions were so totally different from my normal behaviour.

I was, that evening, deeply convicted by God. Embedded within me was the conviction that, if I wronged someone and was aware of that wrong, I needed to go to that person and admit or confess my wrong and ask forgiveness. Up until that evening, I would not, even if I was fully aware of the fact that I was wrong, admit it to anyone, especially the one whom I had personally wronged. From that day forward, I've always made it my goal to confess my wrongdoings, especially to those who are close to me. Although I might not always be aware of the fact that I am wrong, when I am made aware of it I will be the first to admit it. It seems that God surgically removed a scar in my heart that evening, transforming at least one area of my life.

As I've come to know God and his Word more fully, I realize that is the kind of behaviour he desires from his children—not that he expects perfection, as he knows we have been marred by the effects of sin. He only asks that we be honest with ourselves, him, and others, especially those whom we have wronged. He says, *"If we confess our sins he is faithful and just to forgive us our sins and purify us from all unrighteousness"* (1 John 1:9).

I've had to confess many sins to him and to my family over these last thirty-five years. I've had to ask for forgiveness, and I suspect that, knowing myself, I will have to continue to do so. However, in so doing, I am thankful for his forgiveness and, more so, that he is continually doing a work in my heart so that those times seem less frequent. He is the potter and I am the clay and he is shaping me into the image of his son.

I only wish he would hurry it up a bit.

CHAPTER SEVEN
Surprised by Trust

*"Trust in the Lord with all your heart and
lean not on your own understanding; in all
your ways acknowledge him, and he will
make your paths straight."*
(Proverbs 3:5–6)

When I think of trust, I think of dependability or reliability. I think of something or someone on which I can rely to support me and not let me down. It may be a ladder I'm climbing or the branch of a tree I'm standing on, or it may be a person I'm depending on to keep their word. Because of many letdowns in my life, that trust does not often come easily.

One of the fears I overcame that had a huge impact on my trust in God was my fear of water. It happened several years lat-

er, after Cathy had left me and was proceeding to get a divorce. I
had joined a fitness club in order to get in better shape physically and to play racquetball, a sport I had grown to love since I
transferred to a new depot and acquired new friends and coworkers who also loved the sport. The club I joined was located
near my new home and also had a large swimming pool and
sauna. I frequented the club, mostly to play racquetball and enjoy the sauna. I noticed, however, that the pool was seldom used
by the members.

Because it was often empty and I still had not overcome my
fear of water—or more importantly, drowning—I decided to
take advantage of it and first learn to float. I had learned previously, from taking the boys for swimming lessons, that to learn
to swim one first learned to float.

Floating, I had been told, was just a matter of letting the water hold you up due to buoyancy. So, with the desire to overcome my fear of water and finding myself all alone at the pool,
where I wouldn't be embarrassed in a mere two and a half feet of
water, I "waded in," so to speak, to a new learning experience.
Making sure I didn't drift too far out into the pool, I lay down on
my back in the shallow water to see if the water would, in fact,
hold me up. Disappointingly, I found that my legs hung down,
and next thing I knew, my derrière was on the bottom of the
pool. After several attempts at this, and remembering the assurance of acquaintances that the water would hold me up, I decided, quite fearfully, to venture a little deeper. My newfound
courage, however, did not seem to make a difference. My legs

still began to sink, followed by the rest of my body. So, once again, after several vain attempts, and convinced that my body was just not buoyant enough, I gave up.

Several days or weeks later, I was confiding to a friend the unfortunate fact that my body was just not buoyant enough to float. He resolutely assured me that this opinion of mine was not based on fact. He, in his persuasive manner, convinced me to try again, assuring me, in spite of my arguments to the contrary, that I must be trying to hold myself up. He told me to lie down in the water with my head back, just as I would in my own bed. Once again, I went to the pool and endeavoured to trust the water to hold my body up.

This time, following my friend's instructions, I let my head hang back in the water as I would on my own pillow. To my great surprise, I found that, although my legs once again hung down, my body did, in fact, lie prone. I could scarcely believe it. I was floating without any struggle whatsoever.

After several visits with further positive outcomes, I decided to venture further out into the water, at first keeping very close to the edge of the pool. I wanted to be close to safety in case, for some reason or other, I began to sink. As I look back on those times, I am made quite aware that I didn't totally trust the water to hold me up. But as the days and weeks rolled on, so did my confidence in the water to do so. I became braver and started to kick my feet out into the deepest part of the pool, eventually dogpaddling out to the centre and then rolling over onto my back and lying there totally at peace. Knowing deep down that the water was trustworthy, I became more and more comfortable in the water, finally venturing out into lakes twenty to thirty feet deep. Although I have never learned how to swim properly (which, by the way, keeps me from putting my trust in my own abilities), I do make small attempts at it, all the time knowing that I can, at any time, just roll onto my back and let the water take over.

After I came to this assurance of the water's ability to hold me up, the Lord spoke to me one evening about his ability to hold me up in other situations where I had little or no confidence in my own abilities to do so, if only I would just trust him as I did the water. I had been reading about Jesus' reference to end times in Mark's Gospel. Jesus was telling his disciples:

> Whenever you are arrested and brought to trial,
> do not to worry beforehand what to say. Just say
> whatever is given you at the time, for it is not
> you speaking, but the Holy Spirit. (Mark 13:11)

What the Spirit brought home to me while reading that scripture was that I did not have to rely on my own ability but on his ability, just as I didn't have to depend on myself to stay afloat in the water. The more I trusted in him to carry me, the more I could relax and stop striving.

This confidence in God's ability to sustain me has enabled me to venture out of my comfort zone and try many things that I once would have been terrified to try, such as heading up the Hospitality Ministry at our former church, remarrying, adopting a child, heading up the Season Opener at our present church, leading an Alpha Group, becoming a board member of a non-profit society called Luke 15 House that God called me to, and formulating and heading up a large but successful fundraiser for the House—not to mention writing this book!

I had found that, after speaking at the Union Gospel Mission some years before, I would quite often lose track of what I was saying, due to the fact that I tried to follow a prepared script. When I just spoke from my heart regarding the topic that the Lord had placed there, my message seemed to flow better and I was better able to hold my audience's attention. The more I relied on the Lord to guide me and give me the words, the easier the task was.

God was relating to me through the verse in Mark another scripture, which is found in Paul's letter to the Philippians. He said, *"I can do all things through Christ which strengtheneth [enables] me"* (Philippians 4:13, KJV). When I tried to hold myself up in the water, I sank. But when I trusted the water to hold me up, I floated. When I tried to deliver a message according to my own ability, I would stumble and get lost, but when I trusted the Lord to carry me and give me the words, I succeeded. God was showing me that if I put my trust in him, he would provide the means.

So it was that, with that new revelation, I was able to face challenges in my life that would have been extremely difficult, if not impossible, for me if I had to rely on my own abilities.

One such challenge was remarriage. Because of the awareness that my first marriage had failed, in part due to my own weaknesses and inadequacies, I was somewhat afraid to try again. I was aware of those same inadequacies and knew that if I was to succeed in a future relationship, I would need to heavily depend on God to carry me through. I was not certain if it was allowable within God's will for me to remarry at all. But much to my surprise, God had a plan for my life, a plan to give me hope and a future.

CHAPTER EIGHT
Surprised by Providence

"'For I know the plans I have for you,'
declares the Lord, 'plans to prosper you
and not to harm you, plans to give you
hope and a future.'" (Jeremiah 29:11)

Providence, as defined in the Oxford Concise Diction-ary, is "1—the protective care of God or nature, 2—timely care or preparation; foresight; thrift."[9] Thrift, in turn, is defined as "frugality; economical management."[10]

Timely care or preparation, depicted in our lives, could refer to the discipline of our sons and daughters in manners of speech and behaviour in order that when they become adults they in turn have disciplined lives and treat others with respect and dig-

---

[9] Ibid., p. 1102.
[10] Ibid., p. 1453.

nity. Or it could be the setting aside of funds in order that those same children have the means of furthering their education, if they so choose.

Foresight would be the looking ahead to the possible circumstances that one might encounter, such as a leaky roof or a blown engine, or in the case of a farmer, a hailed-out crop, and making preparations or a plan to deal with such eventualities.

Thrift would be the making use of what is available, what one has at one's disposal, in order to make those preparations or carry out one's plans.

As I look once again through the scriptures and the chapters of my life, I see many examples of God's providence, which often reveal themselves in the most surprising ways. One of my favourite stories in the history of Israel, found in the Old Testament, is the story of Joseph. Because of the length of the story, I will only attempt to summarize it. For further understanding, you might do well to read it for yourself, in Genesis 37–45.

Joseph was the great grandson of Abraham, the father of faith and the man who God called out of Haran into a land he didn't know, which is now known as the nation of Israel. Joseph's father was Jacob, the grandson of Abraham, who had twelve sons, Joseph being the eleventh. Although Reuben was the firstborn of the twelve, and due to the customs of the time should have been given the favoured recognition, scripture says:

> Now Israel loved Joseph more than any of his
> other sons, because he had been born to him in
> his old age; and he made a richly ornamented

robe for him. When his brothers saw that their
father loved him more than any of them, they
hated him and could not speak a kind word to
him. (Genesis 37:3–4)

It is interesting to note that Jacob loved Joseph more than
his brothers not only because he was born in Jacob's old age, but
because he was the firstborn of his wife Rachel. To gain more
understanding of the importance of this, I will endeavour to
summarize the story of Jacob, as recorded in Genesis 25–36.

Jacob was the second of twin boys born to Isaac. When he
was a young man, he deceitfully bought the rights of the firstborn from his older twin brother, Esau, and after gaining his father's blessing as the firstborn went to the homeland of his
grandfather Abraham to get a wife from Abraham's relatives. In
his homeland, he met Rachel, the daughter of Jacob's uncle on
his mother's side. His uncle Laban agreed to give his daughter
Rachel to Jacob in marriage on the understanding that he would
work for him for seven years. However, after working those sev-
en years, his uncle Laban gave his oldest daughter, Leah, to him
instead. So Jacob worked for him another seven years in order
to receive Rachel, the one he really loved, in marriage as well.
Rachel was barren, but God gave Jacob six sons through his wife
Leah, and two from Leah's maidservant Zilpah and two from
Rachel's maidservant Bilhah. But then, things changed:

Then God remembered Rachel; he listened to
her and opened her womb. She became preg-

nant and gave birth to a son… She named him
Joseph. (Genesis 30:22–24)

So one of the main reasons Israel loved Joseph more than
any of his other sons was that he was the first to be born to Rachel, his favoured wife. There were, however, other reasons why
his brothers hated him. One was that he gave a bad report about
his brothers to his father. A second reason was the dreams Joseph had, which he shared with his brothers. Both dreams spoke
of his brothers bowing down to him and, in one, even his parents bowed down. So it happened that when Joseph, at his father's request, went out to check on his brothers who were tend-
ing sheep, his brothers, who had a mind to kill him, ended up
selling him as a slave to a passing caravan headed to Egypt. Af-
terward, they took Joseph's robe—first tearing it and then cov-
ering it with blood—back to their father, telling him that they
had found Joseph's robe. Jacob then assumed his young son had
been attacked by an animal and killed.

Meanwhile, things just seemed to get worse for Joseph. He
was bought by Potiphar, the captain of the guard in Egypt.
When Potiphar was away, his wife tried to seduce Joseph. But
because Joseph was a godly man and a loyal servant, he tried to
flee Potiphar's wife. However, she tore off Joseph's robe and
then accused him of trying to sleep with her. Potiphar, in his
anger, had him thrown in prison.

While in prison, Joseph came in contact with the Pharaoh's
chief cupbearer and baker, both of whom had also been impris-
oned. Joseph, in time, had the privilege of interpreting dreams

that both the cupbearer and baker had. Because these interpretations eventually came true, the cupbearer, after he was restored to the Pharaoh's service and heard about troubling dreams the Pharaoh had, informed his master of Joseph and how he was able to interpret dreams.

Therefore, the Pharaoh had Joseph brought out from prison and told him of his dreams. Joseph interpreted the dreams, telling the Pharaoh that they spoke of seven years of plenty that were coming on the land, to be followed by seven years of famine. Joseph then advised the Pharaoh to place a discerning and wise man in charge of the country to build storehouses and collect a fifth of the crops into storage, so that when the seven years of famine arrived there would be plenty of food. The Pharaoh liked Joseph's advice so much that he put him in charge of the country to carry out what Joseph had advised.

When the famine arrived, it not only affected Egypt but the land of Canaan as well. Hence, Jacob and his other sons were also affected. When Jacob heard that there was grain in Egypt, he sent his sons to Egypt to buy some grain. On arriving, they were shown into Joseph's presence but did not recognize him because of the years that had passed and his change in appearance. However, Joseph recognized them and by trickery had them bring his younger brother Benjamin, his mother's son, to him. In the end, Joseph identified himself to his brothers, saying:

> I am your brother Joseph, the one you sold into
> Egypt! And now, do not be distressed and do

not be angry with yourselves for selling me here,
because it was to save lives that God sent me
ahead of you ... So then, it was not you who sent
me here, but God. (Genesis 45:4–5, 8)

What a wonderful example of God's providence! Joseph's
brothers had come to Egypt to purchase food, but to their surprise they were given food for free—and not only food, but the
amazing forgiveness of their brother Joseph and the wonderful
understanding of how God had used them as part of his plan in
providing for the whole family. Because God knew of the famine
that would come upon Egypt and the land of Canaan, he took
timely care and preparation for the provision of Jacob and his
family. God used what was available to get Joseph to Egypt to
prepare for the coming famine: Joseph's jealous and angry
brothers, a caravan on its way to Egypt, an unfaithful wife to his
master, some fellow prisoners with unexplained dreams, the
Pharaoh's own troubling dreams, and finally Joseph's wisdom in
knowing how to handle the upcoming plight.

There are many more examples in scripture that demonstrate God's providence, both in the Old and the New Testament, none of which are as profound as his preparation and
foresight in his plan to redeem his lost people by providing in
his son the path of salvation. However, it is not my purpose to
theologize the scriptures, but to demonstrate how God's involvement in the lives of his people in the past has not changed
from the way he has been and is still involved in my own. This is
proclaimed by God through the prophet Malachi, when he says,

"I the Lord do not change" (Malachi 3:6), and again by the writer of Hebrews, who says, *"Jesus Christ is the same yesterday and today and forever"* (Hebrews 13:8).

One of the ways God has surprised me with his timely care through preparation, foresight, and thrift was in the way he provided me with healing and renewal after my painful divorce from my first wife, Cathy.

The day after God set me free, which I spoke of in the first chapter, he also put it on my heart to renew my vows, this time from my heart. I shared this with my friend George, and he greatly encouraged me to do go through with it.

Thus, several weeks later at our weekly Bible study, our pastor, in the presence of our friends, led us through our vows once again. My vows—"for better, for worse, for richer, for poorer, in sickness and in health, until death do us part, I do give you my troth"—were said this time with conviction. Because of this, I was still very committed to the relationship. In my understanding, my vows were for life, and that understanding only added to the pain of divorce, as it meant that I would be on my own for the rest of my life, unless of course she had a change of mind and decided to come back and renew her vows once again.

As time went on, however, I became more and more uncertain about when that might happen and whether I indeed still wanted it to happen. In my times of deepest pain and despair, I would rant and rave at God, wondering why he was allowing me to go through such pain and whether I was still bound to the marriage or if I could just go on with my life, as many caring friends and pastors were encouraging me to do. I desperately longed for companionship and someone to share my life with, for I had grown up in a large family and had been married with a family for eighteen years. I was finding it very difficult being alone.

After several years, I became tired of spending all my time with only males and decided to seek out female companionship, if only for the purposes of friendship, as I was still uncertain about my relationship with my former wife. I began to date some women who I met through work, friends, or church. None really caught my eye and several became somewhat possessive, at which point I immediately broke off the relationship. At that time, I was really only seeking friendship and not a significant other, due to my uncertainty regarding remarriage.

Around that time, I attended a men's retreat at a home set back near a mountain, several miles from Vancouver. This home was owned and run by a man from our church, and I had attended similar men's retreats there in the past. Reverend Birch, our former pastor, usually led the retreats and was once again involved. However, the studies were led by his associate, David Damien, a former medical doctor from Egypt. Instead of giving us a message, he had us sit in a circle, giving us each twelve pieces of paper and a pencil, as there were twelve men attending. He then asked us to pray quietly in our hearts for each man, one at a time. Before praying, he asked us to write the name of the person we were praying for on one of the pieces of paper and then instructed us to write anything that came to mind as we were praying. It could be, he said, a scripture, a picture, or an event. All we were to do was write it down, no matter how insignificant it seemed.

I do not remember very many of the men who were at the retreat or what came to my mind as I prayed for each of them. What I do remember, to a great degree, is what each of them wrote on the paper as they prayed for me. When we had finished praying for each person and recording on the piece of paper their names and what came to mind as we prayed, he told us to pass the papers to whoever's name was on them. Once we received our collection of papers, he had us take turns sharing what was on each paper.

I was quite amazed at what I read and shared. Three of the men had seen similar pictures and recorded them. They were pictures of two small trees growing side by side. These trees were tied to one another in the same manner a city employee might tie a young tree to a stake in order to support it and help it grow straight. Three or four other men wrote that God was saying that he was going to lead someone into my life. The rest of the men wrote similar words that related to these pictures. What really got my attention was that not only were these bits of information related, but most of the men didn't even know me, never mind my circumstances or the desires of my heart. Only God knew my heart, as I had shared it with him many times, and it was obvious to me that he was giving me a message and confirming it through these men whom I mostly didn't even know.

That weekend really encouraged me, and the chance of once again having a lifelong companion was appearing to be more and more possible. My prayer life started to change from then on. I began telling God about the type of woman I wanted to marry, if in fact he was leading someone into my life. I listed four qualities that were a must for me. The most important thing was that she be a Christian, someone who believed in the goodness and forgiveness of God as I did. She also needed to be open to praying together, hospitable, and someone who loves to give. I also wanted her to be attractive. It was then that I began to watch for who God might bring into my life.

Around that time, I had begun to head up the Hospitality Ministry at our church and could be often found welcoming visitors and handing out bulletins at the main door to the sanctuary. I most often stood there throughout the service, stopping people from entering during prayer. Doing that, I had the distinct advantage of observing the congregation and noticing people now and again who I didn't know. This enabled me to pick out newcomers and, given the chance, welcome them to the church.

One person I noticed was a young lady who reminded me somewhat of a butterfly. She was very colourful and attractive and seemed to have a joyful, light-hearted spirit. I noticed her several Sundays, flitting around from one person to another as a butterfly might flit from one flower to another. The more I saw her, the more interested in her I became and hoped that someone would introduce us at some point, as I was still quite bashful and didn't want to be too forward.

After several weeks had passed and I still had not been introduced, I happened to spot her at a special meeting one Friday evening on the second floor of the building. There was just a small group of people in attendance. I was sitting near the back on the left and she was near the front on the right. I decided that, when the meeting ended, I would approach her and introduce myself.

The moment the meeting was over, I got out of my seat and started to circle around the back in order to meet her. Just then, someone I knew grabbed my shoulder and began speaking to me. I didn't want to be rude, so I listened to what they had to say, all the while keeping an eye on this young lady who was, herself, also chatting with someone. When the person finished what they had to say, I once again proceeded to move towards her. But once again, someone caught my shoulder in order to speak to me. As this person was speaking to me, I noticed her, the center of my attention, start to head for the stairs leading down to the parking lot. This time, not wanting to miss out on the opportunity, I excused myself as graciously as possible and chased her down the stairs. I caught up to her just as she reached the parking lot and awkwardly introduced myself. She cautiously told me her name, Beverly, and then turned and left. Feeling snubbed and embarrassed, I let her leave, not knowing if I would try again.

Some weeks later, there was a church luncheon in the foyer following the service. I was involved at that time with Young Life, a youth ministry that reached out to teens at local high schools. I was a member of the committee for Burnaby-New Westminster and we were at that time organizing, as a fund-raiser, a gift-wrapping event at Eaton Centre Mall in central Burnaby. We were given some tables in the mall at which we could wrap gifts for Christmas shoppers. We supplied the paper and ribbons and set the prices according to the size of the gift. Because the mall was open seven days a week and had longer hours for pre-Christmas shopping, and because there had to be at least two people present at all times, we had a need for many volunteers.

So when I noticed a group of young single women sitting together having lunch, I approached the table, explaining to them what I was doing and asking them if they would consider volunteering for a shift or two of wrapping Christmas gifts for Young Life. Three of them agreed to do so and I got their phone numbers to pass on to the coordinator. One of the three was Beverly. I didn't know it at the time, but she had signed up expecting to be wrapping gifts with me. I had no such intentions and had no idea what shift she was even on. But several weeks later, mustering up my courage once again, I approached her after church one Sunday and asked her what she was doing for lunch. She told me, matter of factly, that she was going out with some friends. I just left it at that, not even asking if I could join them, and began stacking chairs. A friend of mine, who was also helping to stack chairs, asked me what I was doing for lunch. I replied that I had no plans, so he asked me if I wanted to join him.

On arriving at a local Chinese restaurant that was a common meeting place for attendees of our church after the service, I followed him inside to a large table at the back. I didn't know that he was planning to join others and therefore was pleasantly surprised to see Beverly sitting next to me at the table. So it was that we began to chat and get to know one another. She told me that she had been surprised when I was not at the mall wrapping gifts with her and that she had in fact come to know the Lord through the ministry of Young Life. After enjoying a pleasant afternoon lunch together, I asked her if we could have lunch together again sometime soon. She quickly agreed and so our relationship began.

I didn't know it at the time, but Beverly, too, wanted to be remarried. She had been married for a short period of time, but the marriage had ended quite abruptly and she had been on her own for about eight years. She had dated several young men at our church, which explained why I saw her sitting with a variety of people on Sundays. None of those young men seemed suitable to her, however, and she was becoming discouraged. What I also didn't know, until she revealed it to me some months later (after she had accepted my proposal of marriage), was that God had, in his own surprising way, shown her some indication of who he planned to be her partner.

She had, in her discouragement, been telling God one day how she really wanted to be married again. She was dramatically surprised when he said to her, *"Are you willing to let me make the choice this time?"* She was so taken aback by his question that it took her some time to respond to him. However, after thinking about it for a few moments and reflecting on his all-knowing nature, she told him, "Yes."

What happened next surprised her and shocked her. He immediately gave her a picture in her mind of the back of a man's head. What surprised her most about this picture was that the head he showed her was bald on top. She recalled commenting to him, "Does it have to be someone bald?" That wasn't in any way the picture she would have painted for herself; she would have painted a full head of hair and probably someone quite younger than me, as I am almost nine years her senior.

As it turned out, it was shortly after that when I chased her down the stairs and introduced myself. Although that introduction was brief, it was the first step in what would become a relationship that has lasted for more than eighteen years—a relationship that has seen its ups and downs but has grown to be one we both really appreciate. The question is, did we just happen to meet by chance, or did God bring us together supernaturally? It is our belief that it wasn't just a chance meeting but an act of his providence. It was, as we see it, God's timely care, foresight, and thrift.

John said, concerning Jesus, *"To all who received him [as saviour]... he gave the right to become children of God"* (John 1:12).

We are born into his family, and because he is our father we can cast our cares on him because he cares for us. Jesus said, *"Which of you fathers, if your son asks for a fish, will give him a snake instead? Or if he asks for an egg, will give him a scorpion?"* (Luke 11:11–12) Then he adds, *"How much more will your Father in heaven give the Holy Spirit to those who ask him!"* (Luke 11:13) Why? Because he is our father and he cares for us in his own way and time.

Foresight implies that God would have planned our union carefully. As our heavenly father, he would have known each of us, his children, in a most intimate way. He would have been aware of our exact nature, likes and dislikes, temperament, character and passions, faith, commitment, and the deep desires of our hearts. In knowing all this, I believe he would have, in his infinite wisdom, discerned who would, in the multitude of his single children who were yearning to be married, make an ideal match. And then he would have planned how he might bring us together in such a way that we might be joined in marriage.

In my case, he would have known my deep desire to share my life with someone of the opposite sex in a meaningful, open, honest, and committed relationship. He would have known my fear of remaining alone without someone to share my life with. He also would have known about my struggle with the idea of remarriage as it pertained to his will for my life. He would have known the kind of person I wanted to marry if marriage was indeed within his will, and he would have known that she needed to be first of all a woman of faith, one who believed in God, accepted Christ as her Saviour, and shared the same basic beliefs and values as I did—values based on scripture. He would have known that I desired to marry someone who was attractive, beautiful, and pleasing to my eyes, light-hearted and full of life, someone who loved to laugh and have fun, someone who enjoyed hospitality and serving others. He would have known that she would have to be a woman of prayer, of spiritual and sexual intimacy, someone who enjoyed travel and hiking, theatre and reading. And most importantly, he would also have known that she needed to be committed to our relationship and take her marriage vows seriously, vows that spoke of "for better or for worse" and "till death do us part." He would have known this, partly because he knew that was important to me, but mostly because he knew me—my temperament, insecurities, impatience, fears, and still insufficient self-esteem—and that she would need the patience and commitment required to make our marriage work. All these things he would have known, not only because of his divine all-knowing nature, but because I had expressed them to him countless times. I guess I wanted to make sure he had heard me and really understood what I wanted or desired.

In Beverly's case, he would have known her deep desire for family, for fellowship, for both spiritual and sexual intimacy, for loyalty, for trust, and for respect. He would also have known of her mutual desires with regard to faith, prayer, fun, hospitality, and travel. He would have known of her insecurities due to past relationships and her fear of being betrayed as she had been in her first marriage.

Knowing these things and who might make a perfect match, he would have then, in his providence, planned how he might bring us together. And in so doing, he would have used "thrift" (that which was available). In his wisdom and (I believe) fun-loving nature, he would have been sure to use a bucketful of surprises.

In my case, he used a group of men at a men's retreat, most of whom I didn't know, as well as a leader I'd never met before who led us in a demonstration of God's all-knowing and intimate character. When asked to pray for me quietly in their hearts, God had given these same men similar messages about him leading someone into my life. And he not only gave that message to one or two of the men present but to all eleven who were there with me. Again, I must impress, these were men who neither knew me nor the situation I was in, the desires of my heart, or my heartfelt prayers.

He used a variety of mediums, each confirming the other. Talk about surprising! He not only confirmed to me that evening that he was fine with me remarrying but that he was going to lead someone into my life. I was not going to have to go searching for that someone; he was going to lead that person to me. As the pictures of the two trees tied together portrayed, she was going to be someone who would be mutually supportive as we grew in our relationship with him and each other.

As I reflect on that now, I cannot help but be moved by his infinite knowledge, as Beverly has been supportive of me over the last eighteen years of our marriage in so many ways. She has been supportive of my family—both my siblings, their families, and my sons from my first marriage. She has been supportive of my friends from the past and also the strangers I have brought home to spend Christmas or Easter or Thanksgiving with us, strangers I'd met on the bus and who I felt moved by God to invite home, those who had no family to spend the day with, some even of dubious character. She has been supportive of my retirement and my involvement in the church, Luke 15 House, and many other ventures. God knew I needed support and not opposition—because he knew me.

Little did I know that evening at the men's retreat that he had already led the person he had in mind to come to my church looking for a husband. And in order that she didn't overlook me, as she probably would have, he had, in her desperate plea to him for a husband, asked her if she was willing to let him make the choice this time, knowing that she, in her knowledge of him, would say yes. Once he had that commitment from her, he was then able to let her see a part of who that someone was. Knowing her, he knew she would be shocked by what she saw, the back of a man's head. I can almost see the smile on his face and the laughter in his heart as he revealed that image to her.

Also, as a part of his thrift, God had me serving at church in the position where I could not help but see her Sunday after Sunday, observing not only that she was not with anyone in particular but that she was attractive, beautiful, and full of life. Had I not been in that position, I would not have noticed her repeatedly, and therefore I would have bypassed her beauty and joyful spirit.

He had also led each of us to that special meeting on a Friday evening where I would feel more comfortable approaching her. He prompted me to do so, leading to our first real encounter.

And lastly, he used common friends to bring us together, not only to the same restaurant, but to the same table and. More importantly, he seated us next to each other, where we had an opportunity to chat and get to know each other and discover similar interests and our mutual involvement with Young Life.

Do I believe that our relationship was an act of God's providence and not just a coincidental meeting? I most certainly do!

I also believe that the adoption of our son Anthony, who has recently turned nineteen years of age and is now attending Kwantlen College, was also an act of his providence, one by which we've both been blessed beyond measure. We both see him as a gift from heaven, handpicked by our Father, who heard our prayers and knew our desires and our fears and wanted to give us a special gift that was exceedingly and abundantly above all that we could ask or think. And what a gift he has been! He has been an easy child to raise. He bonded with us almost immediately. He has been a delight to have around (at least, most of the time), has been on the Honour Role at school, and is talented, bright, and respectful (again, most of the time). He is well-liked by his peers and, most importantly, by ourselves, as well as our friends and family. Such is the providence of God. Scripture says that he rewards those who diligently seek him.

CHAPTER NINE

Surprised by Revelation

"I did not receive it from any man,
nor was I taught it; rather, I received
it by revelation from Jesus Christ."
(Galatians 1:12)

Once again I will refer to the Concise Oxford Dictionary, this time referring to the word "revelation." It is defined there as "the act or an instance of revealing, esp. the supposed disclosure of knowledge to humankind by a divine or supernatural agency."[11]

I am referring here to God himself, as it is he who has revealed things to me and to the prophets of the Old and New Testaments. I will add here, however, that not all revelation is prophetic. And even if it is, it is not always a foretelling of future

---

[11] Ibid., p. 1178.

events. And neither am I referring to myself as a prophet. But as a child of God, I do receive from him, at times, prophetic words. The first time I was made aware of this was in the late 1970s, while attending Burnaby Christian Fellowship, an offshoot of St. Margaret's Community Church.

When I first attended Burnaby Christian Fellowship on a regular basis, they were meeting in the International Electrical Union Hall. The church rented this hall for Sunday meetings. However, they also rented a small rector house which they used as offices in a neighbouring community. This house was affiliated with a church which had been closed due to a fire and was being rented out until the church could be rebuilt.

Reverend Birch, who was now the pastor of Burnaby Christian Fellowship, held a men's prayer meeting at this house each Saturday morning. These prayer meetings were intended for the men to get to know one another, have fellowship, and pray for the needs of the church and for each other. On one such Saturday morning, he was telling us that he had been asked to speak at a Full Gospel Businessmen's Convention that evening. He then went on to tell us of the problems he had with the leanings of this group of men and asked that we pray for him, that God would reveal to him what it was that he should speak to them about. He had been seeking God for direction as to what to speak about for a few days and as yet had not received any word from him and was becoming concerned, as the event was that evening.

As we began to pray, some were praying out loud requesting that God would indeed reveal to Reverend Birch what it was he would have him speak about. I, mostly because I was timid, was praying quietly in my heart when I became aware of a picture in my mind. In that picture, I saw Reverend Birch standing on a platform in front of a large group of men and women in semi-formal attire sitting around tables, speaking to them about the very concerns that he had expressed to us.

After we had finished praying, I got up the nerve to tell them about the picture I had while praying. Reverend Birch thanked me and the following morning one of the elders of the church who had been at the prayer meeting approached me to tell me that what I had shared was prophetic. He informed me that Reverend Birch had indeed spoken about the things which had concerned him and his message had been well-received by those who attended, as well as by those in charge of the event.

Another time, just three or four years ago, a couple from our church attended a Bible study at our home one Sunday evening. They were the only ones who came that evening and were attending for the first time. At the end of the evening, I asked if there was anything they would like prayer for. The lady, we'll call her Louise, said that she had become worn down because of the busyness and stress of her life. She worked at the University of British Columbia heading up the coordination of foreign students and was also in the process of studying for her Master's Degree. She was also having stress-related difficulties with some relatives who were expected to arrive that week. She then had to fly to Toronto the same week to be the presenter at a conference there. She was stressed about this conference, as it would be the first time she had done anything like that before. She was feeling quite overwhelmed by it all and asked for prayer.

As we prayed for her, a hymn that I hadn't heard for some years suddenly began playing in my mind. Because of the way it unexpectedly came to me, and being aware of how God seems to surprise me with words and pictures, I had to believe it was from God. The hymn, entitled "Showers of Blessings," began with the words:

> There shall be showers of blessings.
> This is the promise of love.
> There shall be seasons refreshing,
> Sent from the Saviour above.[12]

As these words began playing in my mind, I trusted they were for Louise and decided to share with her what I believed God was saying. I asked her if she was familiar with the song and she replied no. I repeated these lines to her and then got out my hymnal and let her read and reflect on the words and chorus. She left that evening feeling rather enthused.

The next time I spoke with her, I asked how the visit and travel had gone. She was totally excited and told me that by believing God was going to bless her she had been able to relax. Both the visit from her relatives and her first-time presentation

---

[12] Redemption Hymnal (Eastbourne, East Sussex, UK: Kingsway Publications, 1951), #245.

went incredibly well. She told me that she had been totally blessed. Knowing that the word I shared with her had come from God and that it had been fulfilled, I knew that God had once again given me a prophetic word.

Revelations, however, are not always predictive. In my case, they seldom are. They are more often words, pictures, visions, songs, scripture, dreams, or interpretations of dreams that reveal to us an awareness of things that are beyond our own ability to know. They often disclose knowledge, as the above definition of revelation suggests, and come as a result of a request to God about a particular situation. For me, they are most often surprising, just as the two above examples were. The more I've come to recognize God's ways of speaking to me and to trust these revelations, the more often I receive them, or at least am made aware of them. All of these revelations, to me, are profound in their scope. I have already mentioned several of these cases, but there are two more that I would like to make mention of. Both of these revelations occurred just after my divorce.

The first happened before the Christmas after Cathy and I sold our home in Burnaby. I was renting a townhouse close to where we had once lived, one which I shared with a good friend of mine who was also divorced. As I recall, our youngest son was living with me at the time and our oldest was living with his mother. Thinking ahead, I had called Cathy to ask her if she wanted to get together for Christmas. She told me she would think about it and get back to me. Several days later, she called and said that it would be fine. She asked me if I would buy the turkey and, if so, she would cook it at her place and we could have dinner there. I had agreed to that and arrangements were made for her to pick up the turkey on the morning of Christmas Eve. She told me that she was getting off work early that day and, as my place was nearby her work and I had time off during the day, she would pick it up on her way home.

As I was working split-shifts at the time, arrangements were made for her to come over around ten o'clock in the morning, after I had returned from the first part of my shift. When she arrived, I was in the middle of stuffing the turkey and offered her a cup of coffee. She had brought along some of her wash, as I had a washer and dryer in my suite and she did not. She asked if she could use my machines. I told her it was fine and, as the washing was in progress, we drank coffee and chatted. While chatting, I was made distinctly aware of a heavy presence about her. She left around noon, all the time looking worn-out and stressed.

As I was feeling rather tired myself and had a long day ahead of me—I still had some shopping to do, the rest of my shift to complete, and dinner arrangements to attend with some good friends who had invited me over for Christmas Eve—I decided that I would stretch out on the living room sofa while I made a list of items I wanted to purchase before going back to work. As I completed my list and was reflecting on Cathy's condition, I said to God, somewhat offhandedly, that I would also like to get some small thing for her that would make her feel special. I had already purchased a gift certificate for her at The Bay, but due to the awareness of her present state, I had compassion on her and wanted to get her something else that might lift her spirits.

As I look back on that afternoon, I can't help but think that it was a good thing I was laying down. What God revealed to me so surprised me that I believe I might have otherwise fallen down. For immediately he showed me a picture in my mind of a neon sign with the word "diamond" flashing in bold letters. The idea of a diamond was totally beyond what I would have thought of and totally beyond the price of what I was thinking of. My words, "some small thing," had also included the thought "some small price."

I was totally shocked, but as I reflected on the word diamond, I realized that it was in fact quite small and would in fact make her—or any woman, for that matter—feel special. Because of the surprising uniqueness of the picture I'd received, I knew that this had to be from God and definitely not from my own mind. So I said to him, "If this is from you, you're going to have to help me find one that's not too expensive."

Being aware of the time, I decided to get going, as I didn't have a lot of time to go shopping and then be at work at two-thirty in Port Coquitlam, which was a good twenty-minute drive away. As I got my things together for work, I was telling God that I didn't want to spend a lot of money and was not sure how expensive diamonds were, never having been in the position of buying one. As I did so, the figure of $250 came into my mind, a figure I thought was manageable, as well as the word "Mappins." I was not sure if that was the name of a jewellery store or not, but I had some small recollection of having seen that name somewhere. As I headed out the door, the word "pendant" also came to me. As well, I had a picture of some short pieces of string lying in a box, coupled with the thought, "No strings attached." I was not sure if any of these thoughts were from God or just thoughts flitting through my mind, but I knew that I had to presume they were from God and move in that direction.

As I approached our local mall and looked for a parking spot, I was not able to find one, as they all appeared to be filled. Several times I spotted someone leaving the mall, heading for the parking lot. I would immediately try to get into the lane they were headed for in order to acquire the spot they would vacate. Each time I failed, as there was always another vehicle that beat me there. After about ten to fifteen minutes of this, and realizing my limited time, I once again spoke to God and said, "If this is from you, you are going to have to help me find a parking spot."

Those words no sooner left my mouth than I received another picture, this time of an empty parking spot right in front of the door to a new section of the mall around the corner, a door which I had never entered before. I proceeded in that direction, and as I turned the corner I saw a vehicle leaving a parking spot directly in front of the door that had just been pictured in my mind. Now I was really excited as I parked my vehicle and hurriedly entered the door.

Remembering the word "Mappins" and not knowing if there was such a place, or if there was whether it was in the mall or not, I immediately inquired of the first store I saw after entering.

It was a Purdy's Chocolate store. I approached the counter, asking the person behind it if there was a Mappins Jewellers in the mall. She said she didn't know, and I turned to leave and ask someone at the next store. Just as I turned, another lady working there responded, telling me that it was on the second floor near The Bay. At this, I recalled a jewellery store being there and headed in that direction. As I entered Mappins Jewellery, which was quite busy because of the season, a female clerk near the back of the store, who saw me coming in, shouted to me, "I have just what you are looking for."

I headed in her direction and she showed me a pair of diamond earrings that were on sale for $250. I was amazed and was about to purchase them when I remembered the word "pendant." Not entirely sure what a pendant was, I asked the clerk whether she had any diamond pendants. She assured me they did and asked me to head back near the front of the store, where she showed me two. The second one she showed me was a heart-shaped pendant with a diamond in the middle suspended from a gold chain. As soon as I saw it, I knew it was the right one, for not only was it 50% off and priced at $249.99, but I was reminded of a request Cathy had made the day we moved out of the house we had shared together—she had asked me to keep an eye out for her gold chain as I cleaned up the house before turning over possession to the new owner. This was my opportunity to "replace" that lost item.

The clerk offered to wrap it for me. I agreed, as it would save me time and I still had other shopping to do before returning to work. I left the jewellery store and proceeded to other stores to pick up the remaining items on my list. I was able to accomplish this task in unbelievable time and got to work with time to spare. In my rush, the only thing I did not do was have some short pieces of string put in the case with the diamond pendant, which was the one part of the revelation I did not complete.

As I look back on that remarkable afternoon, I am always astounded by the incredible riches of God's grace and his unfathomable wisdom and knowledge—this grace given to Cathy, who had pursued a divorce in spite of the counsel of her counsellor, workmates, and others, and the grace given to me by responding to my desire to bless Cathy and leading me to the ideal gift, thus encouraging me that he was not only there for me, but also able to do exceedingly, abundantly above all I could ask or think. As scripture says, *"If God is for us, who can be against us?"* (Romans 8:31)

The second revelation happened some time the following year. I was still working out of the Port Coquitlam garage and was still working split-shifts. My friend Lawrence was still living with me and I was still hurting from the loss, rejection, and sense of betrayal by my partner and wife.

On a Thursday evening during dinner, Lawrence told me that Doug, my old friend and neighbour, had called. After dinner, I phoned Doug to find out why he had called. His wife Gerry answered the phone, and after I asked to speak to Doug she informed me that he had gone out. When I inquired if she knew the reason for his call, she said it was his night to go to the Union Gospel Mission the following Monday and he had probably been calling to see if I would go with him.

The next evening, while on my way home from work, I was talking to God about my need to call Doug. I said to him, "Doug probably wants me to go to the Mission. If he does, I am willing to go, but if he wants me to share I am going to have to say no, as I've got nothing to share. I feel totally empty."

I had no sooner spoken these words in my heart when a chorus I had not sung in years began playing in my mind. Because it simply came out of the blue and surprised me, I immediately realized this had to be from God. And as I reflected on the words—*"The Lord is my portion, sayeth my soul, therefore shall I hope in him"*—I was able to discern that the words were scriptural. But I was not able to grasp the meaning of them. However, knowing that if they were from God he would have had a purpose in giving them to me, I decided to get my concordance out when I got home.

Not knowing if the words were scripture or only based on scripture, and not having any idea where they might be found in the Bible, I picked the word "portion" and looked it up in the concordance. As the word is not often used in the Bible, I found the reference quite easily in the book of Lamentations. The passage was word-for-word in line with the chorus, but after reading it and several verses before and after, I was still not able to comprehend its meaning. I began to struggle with the word "portion," and as I did so I saw a circle, as in the shape of a pie, cut into portions. The bottommost portion had the word

"Lord" written on it. That got me thinking as to what the other portions might be. Knowing that the book of Lamentations was written by the prophet Jeremiah, and that it was he who was saying *"The Lord is my portion,"* I began to wonder what other peoples' portions in life were.

As I thought about this, the first thing that came into my mind was a *name*. Some people's portion in life is the name they were born with, such as Prince Charles or Prince Edward. They did nothing to earn that name, but simply received it at birth. As I thought about myself, I was quite aware that it was definitely not my portion in life. I was just a farm boy from the prairies. No one would even know I existed unless they met me or were told about me by a friend or relative. I was simply one of the many "nobodies" in the world.

Then I thought of those who were known for their wisdom, like Albert Einstein. Again, I knew that I was definitely not in that category. I was not very bright, in my opinion at least, and had in fact not even graduated from high school.

Then I thought about riches. There are people who are known for their riches. Some are merely born into riches while others acquire it, whether by honest means or deceit, or by hard work or inheritance. I knew that I did not fit in that category, either. I had just sold our house and had a little money in the bank, but I was definitely not rich, at least not in our environment.

Suddenly the portions began to fill in, as my mind geared to the whole idea. I thought of strength, such as that of Sampson from Bible times, or in our day, Hossien Reza Zadeh, who won both the 2000 and 2004 gold medal in weightlifting at 472.5 pounds. Once again, it did not come near to a description of myself. I had just had, a short time before, a fitness test at work and was informed by the attending instructor that I lacked muscle content for my age and height, a result of my having being a bus driver for several years. This was one of the reasons I had joined the fitness club I mentioned earlier.

"Talent" was the next word to fill in a portion of the pie. Great musicians, actors, and athletes came to mind. That definitely didn't have anything to do with me, either. I had no talents that I was aware of. Sure, I could drive a bus, but who couldn't?

As I completed the pie, I now knew what Jeremiah meant when he said, *"The Lord is my portion."* The Lord was my portion as well. What a revelation! A revelation that was humbling, I must say, but a revelation nonetheless. That was only the beginning of the revelation, however. I thought, *All I have is the Lord*, and let that settle in my mind. Then the Lord began to show me that in him I had all the rest as well.

I had a name, because my father not only made the world as we know it, but he owns it as well. Everything is his. I am, in fact, a son of the Most High.

As a child of God, I also possess wisdom and riches. Our father gives us wisdom; we need only ask. He also gives us riches, sometimes earthly riches and sometimes not. But he definitely gives us heavenly riches, such as peace, joy, love, freedom, and

more. And to top it all off, I have a rich inheritance waiting for
me in heaven, an inheritance that is mine because of the surpass-
ing grace that he bestowed on us through his son Jesus Christ.

Furthermore, he gives me strength to face up to my fears,
my weaknesses, and my failures. And lastly, he has given me talents. I was born with them, as are you. We only need to discover
them, and he helps us do that if we allow it. It surprises me to
find some of the talents that have been hidden away in me just
waiting to be discovered.

Just then, I remembered I needed to call Doug back, so I
proceeded to do so. It was no surprise when he asked me to join
him the following Monday to go to UGM. Nor was it a surprise
for him to ask me if I could share something with the men and
women there at the Mission. What was a surprise, however, was
that due to the revelation I'd just received, I was able to say yes
to both requests, for not only had God given me an understanding of what I have in him, but he also gave me a message to
share.

And talk about surprises! My interest being piqued by the
surprising but short chorus that had popped into my head, I was
led on a hunt to the remarkable discovery of my inheritance in
him, a revelation that filled me with hope, peace, gratitude, and
joy.

What a revelation it was, one of such magnitude that I might
compare it to a poor, downtrodden beggar following a rainbow
and being led to that legendary pot of gold. I had been telling
God how empty I'd felt and his response was, in the most sur-

prising way, not only to fill that emptiness but at the same time to lead me to an understanding of who I was in Christ, giving me a new sense of significance and worth. Such is the greatness, character, compassion, ingenuity, and love of God.

> For this is what the high and lofty One says—he who lives forever, whose name is holy: "I live in a high and lofty place, but also with him who is contrite and lowly in spirit, to revive the spirit of the lowly and to revive the heart of the contrite." (Isaiah 57:15)

I must say, he most certainly revived my heart, and he can revive yours, too, if you will only humble yourself before him and seek his face.

CHAPTER TEN

Surprised by Wisdom

"For the Lord gives wisdom, and from his mouth come knowledge and understanding." (Proverbs 2:6)

A s the above verse implies, true wisdom comes from God. It is a gift, and according to scripture it is given freely and generously to anyone who asks. The one who asks for it, however, must first be willing to trust God's Word that has been imparted. For if he or she doesn't trust, he or she will become unstable and, as scripture says, be like a wave of the sea, blown and tossed by the wind.

I had the fortunate privilege of receiving from God a revelation, that the Bible was indeed the Word of God, filled with the wisdom of God and the purpose of God. And because of that revelation, my pursuit of wisdom began.

However, due to my limited knowledge of life and my inability to trust God, the first several years of my Christian walk were quite unstable. My life was similar to a rollercoaster ride, subject to thrilling highs followed by scary and frightening dives into uncertainty and doubt.

Two things helped me through those turbulent years. One was the direct revelations from God regarding his love and faithfulness to me, and secondly, the availability and wisdom of my pastor, Reverend Birch. Reverend Birch was to me, at that time, my teacher and private tutor, so to speak. Besides listening to his sermons each week, which were filled with wisdom, he made himself available to me and a host of others to hear our struggles and give us a godly word of wisdom in response. It never failed to amaze me how he could, after listening to my ramblings for several minutes at a time, give a brief but simple word of wisdom that would calm the storm that was raging in my mind and set me at ease once again.

I felt much like a student who was facing a page full of math problems with no idea how to solve them, but who was able to find comfort and get through them with the help of his tutoring. I must say, Reverend Birch's method of tutoring was to listen to the problem and seek God for wisdom, which was most often, if not always, a scripture. He would then point out to me what I needed to do. Most often, what he conveyed to me was a confirmation of what I believed God had been saying to me in the first place, but due to my lack of trust in my ability to hear or recognize God's voice, coupled with the unbelief of others in that same ability, I didn't have the confidence to act on the word I believed I had heard. So it was that after several times of coming to my pastor to share with him what I believed God was telling me, he responded one evening with these words: "You are double-minded." Then he went on to explain by quoting James' letter, which refers to people who are double-minded. James, in effect, says that if you ask God for wisdom, he will give it—so don't doubt it when you receive it. For when you doubt what you've asked for in faith, you are double-minded, only trusting God enough to ask but not trusting when you get the answer.

Reverend Birch has long since left that church and has now, in his old age, left this world to be with the Lord. But what he imparted to me was a confidence that I, as one of God's sheep, one of his adopted children, can hear his voice and receive wisdom from him.

One of the first times I can remember hearing God clearly on my own in response to a cry over a dilemma I found myself in came in my early years as a Christian. I was a parent to two young boys at the time, and due to the fact that I was trying to be a good and responsible parent, I had read a book called *Dare to Discipline*.[13] The book, written by Dr. James Dobson, dealt with the need for a parent to discipline in love. One of the significant passages that spoke to me was the matter of following through on your word. Dr. Dobson states clearly that if you don't follow through on your word, you are in fact implying that

---

[13] Dobson, Dr. James. *Dare to Discipline* (Wheaton, IL: Tyndale House Publishing, 1970).

your words have no bearing on reality—that your threats are meaningless.

At the time, I was being challenged in many respects by our youngest son, Derek. He was a very intelligent and outgoing boy, but also a very strong-willed child. Unfortunately, because of my lack of parenting skills, I had instilled in him the idea that I did not stand by my word. But after reading *Dare to Discipline*, I was determined to change that. And so began an array of disciplines with Derek. I had grounded him from sports activities because of his non-compliance regarding our request that he let us know where he was and get our permission before going off to play with friends after school. I had also grounded him from television for a period of time for not completing his homework, of which, most often, he insisted he had none.

Now I was telling him that if he didn't feed and water the rabbits he kept in a cage in our backyard, he would either have to sell them or give them away. I was not going to stand by and watch them die of either hunger or thirst. Furthermore, I was determined to have Derek follow through on his promises. Again, this was an uphill battle, due to my letting him and his brother Raymond slide in regards to keeping former promises with our pet dog, Sparky.

We had acquired Sparky through a neighbour of friends of ours. He was a cross between a Husky, a Collie, and a Terrier. We had prayed as a family for a dog that would be selected and provided by God. And what a selection! Both boys, now men, still talk about Sparky and what a great dog he was. Previously, we had owned a dog by the name of Cuddles, but Cuddles had been run over by a neighbour on our cul-de-sac. Cathy had been so grieved by the loss of Cuddles that she had not wanted to get another pet. However, the boys missed having a dog and conspired together to get one. After much pleading, they drew up and agreed to a list of promises if only we would let them have one. They had promised to feed it, train it, bathe it, brush it, and take it for walks along with a multitude of other things I can no longer recall. So, after much pleading on their part and some persuasion on mine, Cathy finally agreed to it, so we prayed for the ideal pet.

But after having it for a few weeks and the duties of owning a pet grew weary, I gradually found it much easier to feed, brush, and walk the dog myself rather than to have to keep reminding and overseeing the boys.

Now we had two rabbits. A neighbour and friend of Derek's had sold him a rabbit. It was a miniature rabbit that he had given the name Squirt. It was a cute little rabbit and he was allowed to keep it only if he looked after it. I was determined this time not to get involved in the care of it. So Derek took on the responsibility of doing so. He purchased a second-hand cage and each morning and afternoon took the rabbit out of the cage to feed on grass and carrots in the backyard and to give it water to drink. Unfortunately, the rabbit lasted only a week or two before passing away. None of us knew that a tame rabbit needed special rabbit pellets to eat, and because of that he died. Derek was overcome with grief as well as anger towards God for letting the

rabbit die. I had compassion on him and we gave it a proper bur-
ial in the backyard.

After informing his friends of the rabbit's death, they explained to him why it had happened (improper diet) and offered him another rabbit. He told me it just wasn't the same, as
this rabbit wasn't anything like Squirt—it was much larger, for
one thing. However, after much persuasion by his friends and
me advising that it would help him get over the loss of Squirt, he
took it. As I look back now, it probably wasn't the best advice.
However, at the time I thought it was wise and so began the new
challenge of getting him to look after it. His brother Raymond
decided he would like one also and agreed to take turns buying
the food and supplying both food and water.

Unfortunately, due to the responsibility of looking after it
falling mostly on Raymond, he sold his rabbit to his younger
brother, who then had two. It was shortly after this that I told
Derek of his need to either sell the rabbit or give it away if he
was not prepared to tend to its needs. It got to the point where
he was only allowed one reminder a week, or he would have to
get rid of it. That happened on a Sunday and the following few
days he seemed to have gotten the message, as when I checked
the cage on returning home from work the rabbit had both food
and water.

But on Wednesday evening when I checked, there was no
water or food in the cage. At dinner that evening, I asked him if
he had fed the rabbits and he quickly responded that he had forgotten and was quick to go out and do so. And I was quick to

remind him of my promise concerning there being only one reminder.

On the following two days, it was evident that the rabbits were being taken care of and I was pleased that he was taking me and his responsibilities seriously. However, on the following Saturday, I was asked to work late and didn't return until 9:30 p.m. When I got home, it was dark, but with the help of a flashlight I checked the cage only to find they had neither food nor water. As he was already in bed, I waited until the following morning to inquire as to whether he had fed and watered them.

I was in the bathroom shaving for church the next morning when he came up from his room and plunked himself down on the chesterfield in the living room. As I had not closed the door to the bathroom and had a clear view of the living room, I saw him arrive. Without waiting to finish shaving, I walked out into the living room and asked him, "Derek, did you feed and water the rabbits yesterday?" I was inwardly hoping, in spite of my doubts, that he had and that the rabbits had finished it all before I got home. However, Derek, being quite honest, said he hadn't and I, quite frustrated, said, "You know what that means?" His response was dramatic, with just a solemn nod and then a drooping of his head and a sigh.

I left him and went back to shaving, feeling like a harsh and unfair parent. I was acutely aware of the fact that he was grounded from television, sports, and his friends... and was now forced to sell or give away his rabbits. With tears starting down my cheeks and the razor still in hand, I looked to God and said,

"Lord, I don't know what to do!" I was caught in a dilemma—either I had to be an overly harsh parent or I had to go back on my word. I was torn apart inside, as I did not want to do either.

But no sooner had I uttered those words than God responded, in his still small voice, with these words, *"You buy them."* Suddenly, I realized that God, in his wisdom, had provided a solution. I had told Derek that he either had to sell them or give them away, and here I was given the simple but profound solution: *"You buy them."* What a relief to my grieving heart and what an opportunity to save face.

I immediately went out to the living room and asked him how much he had paid for the rabbits. When he told me the amount—only a few dollars—I reached into my pocket and pulled out my wallet, paying him the price for the rabbits. Feeling relieved as a parent, I then told him that I was returning them to him and giving him another chance.

The following morning, after sharing this story to our congregation in response to the message of hearing the Word of God, one of the elders came up to me and said, "That is the Gospel." I hadn't thought of that, but as I reflected on it, I realized that what he said was true. For just as we warrant the penalty of death (eternal separation from God), God in his mercy paid the price by sending his son to die in our place. He paid the price that we might have life again. Until then, I had not seen the significance of my actions, which were, of course, a response to God's wisdom.

I could go on to tell you of many countless times when God has given me wisdom when faced with difficult decisions or circumstances, but I do not feel the need to do so. My purpose is to disclose that God himself is the holder of ultimate wisdom and knowledge and that he can impart that wisdom to you or to me if only we ask in faith. I say in faith, because firstly, we won't ask for it if we don't first believe that he exists and knows all things, and secondly, we have to receive and trust the wisdom he gives us and act upon it. In so doing, we will be surprised not only by his wisdom but by the manner in which he imparts it to us. He not only knows all things, but he knows our limited understanding and how best to deliver what we need in a manner that we personally can understand, and often he does this in *surprising* ways. How unsearchable are his truths!

As the above story illustrates, he imparted wisdom to me by his quiet inner voice within me, his Holy Spirit. Quite often, that is the way he speaks to me, but most often he speaks through his Word, the Bible, although at other times it is through visions or dreams, through my brothers and sisters in Christ, through books, or maybe even nature itself. How great is our God!

Am I saying that I am wise? By no means! I constantly need to seek him for wisdom in difficult situations in my life—and quite often for the same reason more than once, as I am quick to forget what he has already told me. I seem to be such a slow learner, but nevertheless I *am* learning. And the most important lesson I am learning is that God, in his wisdom, is an everpresent help in time of need.

One pearl of wisdom that God imparts to his people through his Word is found in the book of Jeremiah. In speaking to his people through Jeremiah, he says,

> Let not the wise man boast in his wisdom or the strong man boast in his strength or the rich man boast of his riches, but let him who boasts boast about this: that he understands and knows me, that I am the Lord, who exercises kindness, justice and righteousness on earth, for in these I delight. (Jeremiah 9:23–24)

Do I know and understand God? Only partly. But the more I get to know him, the more I want to know him; the more I want to know him, the more I seek him; and the more I seek him, the more he reveals to me about himself. It's a win-win scenario.

And you, too, can get to know him if you so choose. He is no respecter of persons, for he wants all mankind to be saved and come to the knowledge of the truth. You need only believe that he exists, turn to him with a repentant heart, confess your hidden sins to him, and ask him for forgiveness.

Epilogue

Life is full of surprises. Many are heart-warming, inspiring, re-freshing, and uplifting. On the other hand, some are painful, dis-appointing, and downright discouraging. What have you been surprised by lately? Has it been a substantial inheritance from a distant relative? A lottery win? The start of a new and wonderful relationship? On the other hand, has it been the sudden death of a loved one? The diagnosis of cancer? A tornado or fire that has destroyed your place of refuge?

Whatever the surprise, and no matter what package it is wrapped in, I have come to discover that it may be a gift from God. Surprises that are bright, inspiring, and encouraging can easily be recognized as coming from him if one knows him. Surprises that are wrapped in pain, however, are not so easily accepted. Though such surprises may bring discomfort and pain into your life, they can sometimes be the most precious gifts you can receive, as it is often through these gifts that we grow the most.

My divorce from my first wife, Cathy, was one of those gifts. Although it was probably the most painful and difficult time I have ever experienced, when I look back I am thankful for it, as it helped me grow as a person and my life has become richer since. The destitution of soul that resulted from my lack of freedom and understanding of life was what led me to my knowledge of God and his love for me, the best gift I've ever received. Scripture says that all things work together for good for those who love God and are called according to his purpose.

If you already know the Lord as your saviour, you have been called by him. And if you don't, it just may be that God is calling you now. Either way, it is my hope that you may be surprised to discover, as I did, that God is there for you in the midst of both the uplifting as well as the disappointing and painful; he is able to work both together for good. He is a loving father who wants to encourage and strengthen you, bring healing in your brokenness and to rejoice with you in your victories. Like the sun, he is always present, abounding with love. And like the water, he is faithful to uphold you in any circumstance if you will but put your trust in him.

It is my hope that, in reading my story, you have been encouraged and inspired to do just that—to put your trust in God if you haven't already done so. You need only turn to him, confess your shortcomings and failures, and ask his forgiveness and he will, as his Word states, forgive your sins and cleanse you of all unrighteousness. Be truthful with him, for he already knows everything about you and wants only to help you overcome your weaknesses and build into you a stronger and more fruitful character. And, surprisingly, he will do just that, for he loves you more than you can ever imagine and wants you to be a part of his life. Seek his face and get to know the God of surprises and of love, for he is the rewarder of those who earnestly seek him.

If you, however, already know God and have a relationship with him, I hope my story may encourage you to trust his unchanging love for you even more than you already have. I hope that you will be inspired to spend more time with him in prayer and in the reading his Word, that you will deepen your relationship with him and learn to recognize his voice more clearly, and that you may get to know him better so that your soul will be stilled and quieted within you. You, too, may be surprised to discover just how much he truly loves you.

In conclusion, I will leave you with one of David's psalms which captures the heart of what this book is all about:

> I will exalt you, my God the King;
> I will praise your name for ever and ever.
> Every day I will praise you and extol your name
> for ever and ever.
>
> Great is the Lord and most worthy of praise; his
> greatness no one can fathom.
> One generation will commend your works to
> another; they will tell of your mighty acts.

They will speak of the glorious splendor of your
   majesty, and I will meditate on your
   wonderful works.
They will tell of the power of your awesome
   works, and I will proclaim your great deeds.
They will celebrate your abundant goodness
   and joyfully sing of your righteousness.

The Lord is gracious and compassionate, slow
   to anger and rich in love.
The Lord is good to all; he has compassion on
   all he has made.
All you have made will praise you, O Lord; your
   saints will extol you.
They will tell of the glory of your kingdom and
   speak of your might, so that all men may
   know of your mighty acts and the glorious
   splendor of your kingdom.
Your kingdom is an everlasting kingdom, and
   your dominion endures through all
   generations.

The Lord is faithful to all his promises and
   loving toward all he has made.
The Lord upholds all those who fall and lifts up
   all who are bowed down.
The eyes of all look to you, and you give them
   their food at the proper time.
You open your hand and satisfy the desires of
   every living thing.

The Lord is righteous in all his ways and loving
   toward all he has made.
The Lord is near to all who call on him, to all
   who call on him in truth.
He fulfills the desire of those who fear him; he
   hears their cry and saves them.
The Lord watches over all who love him, but all
   the wicked he will destroy.

My mouth will speak in praise of the Lord.
Let every creature praise his name for ever and
   ever.
(Psalms 145:1–21)

IF you have questions,
email me at allanmoff@gmail.
com with subject:
        your book